DD769719

"Brimming with wise counsel, practical
pose, this excellent guide transcends all
for not only parents but teachers as well.

— ARCHIBALD D. HART, PhD, FPPR, dean emeritus and
senior professor, Graduate School of Psychology,
Fuller Theological Seminary

"If you are a parent who wants a more respectful relationship with
your child, study Dr. Cartmell's book and practice the ideas together.
This book is a concise and accessible guide to better parent-child
interaction."

— ANITA E. STAUFFER, PhD

"This book is a well-written, systematic, biblical, and practical
approach to teaching our children respect. The "Key Points to
Remember" and "Taking the Next Step" sections are very helpful.
I enjoyed reading it and think this book is a must-read for every
parent."

— DIANE NIELSON, MD, private practice pediatrician

"Dr. Cartmell's revolutionary new approach takes child training far
beyond simple obedience and discipline, getting right to the heart
of the matter: teaching your child respect. The crucial skills learned
here will truly bring out the best in your child today and for a life-
time. What an invaluable resource!"

— KATHLEEN PETIT, mother of seven

Respectful Kids

The Complete Guide to Bringing Out the Best in Your Child

Dr. Todd Cartmell

NAVPRESS®

BRINGING TRUTH TO LIFE

OUR GUARANTEE TO YOU

We believe so strongly in the message of our books that we are making this quality guarantee to you. If for any reason you are disappointed with the content of this book, return the title page to us with your name and address and we will refund to you the list price of the book. To help us serve you better, please briefly describe why you were disappointed. Mail your refund request to: NavPress, P.O. Box 35002, Colorado Springs, CO 80935.

The Navigators is an international Christian organization. Our mission is to advance the gospel of Jesus and His kingdom into the nations through spiritual generations of laborers living and discipling among the lost. We see a vital movement of the gospel, fueled by prevailing prayer, flowing freely through relational networks and out into the nations where workers for the kingdom are next door to everywhere.

NavPress is the publishing ministry of The Navigators. The mission of NavPress is to reach, disciple, and equip people to know Christ and make Him known by publishing life-related materials that are biblically rooted and culturally relevant. Our vision is to stimulate spiritual transformation through every product we publish.

ISBN 1-57683-984-2

Cover design by David Uttley, www.thedesignworksgroup.com
Cover photo by Photonica
Creative Team: Terry Behimer, Arvid Wallen, Laura Barker, Cara Iverson, Kathy Guist

Names and specific details regarding the children and families described in this book have been carefully altered to protect their privacy.

All Scripture quotations in this publication are taken from the HOLY BIBLE: NEW INTERNATIONAL VERSION® (NIV®). Copyright © 1973, 1978, 1984 by International Bible Society. Used by permission of Zondervan Publishing House. All rights reserved.

Library of Congress Cataloging-in-Publication Data
Cartmell, Todd, 1962-
  Respectful kids : the complete guide to bringing out the best in your
child / Todd Cartmell.
     p. cm.
  Includes bibliographical references.
  ISBN 1-57683-984-2
  1. Child rearing--Religious aspects--Christianity. 2.
Parenting--Religious aspects--Christianity. I. Title.
  BV4529.C427 2006
  248.8'45--dc22
                              2006012341

Printed in the United States of America

1 2 3 4 5 6 / 10 09 08 07 06

FOR A FREE CATALOG OF NAVPRESS BOOKS & BIBLE STUDIES,
CALL 1-800-366-7788 (USA) OR 1-800-839-4769 (CANADA)

Contents

Acknowledgments

I am so grateful to Lora, Jacob, and Luke for being the best family that any husband and dad could hope to have in a thousand lifetimes. I am also deeply indebted to my editor, Laura Barker, for her relentless attention to detail and devoted efforts to help me communicate these ideas in the most effective way possible.

I'd like to dedicate this book to my father, whose amazing faith and integrity are a constant example of how to walk with God through life's mountains and valleys.

R-E-S-P-E-C-T, Find Out What It Means to You

getting to the heart of the matter

It was a sunny April afternoon in Dayton, Ohio, with winter clearly behind us and the freshness of spring bursting all around. My two-year-old son, Jacob, had been enjoying his chance to once again roll down the grass hill behind our small apartment. After our little human bowling ball had managed to secure grass stains over every square inch of his body, my wife, Lora, who was every bit of eight months pregnant with our second son, decided to take Jacob to his favorite restaurant, McDonald's. What a mom!

When they arrived at the Golden Arches, Lora ordered a Chicken McNuggets Happy Meal for Jacob (and a Quarter Pounder with cheese and large fries for herself). As they sat down to eat, Jacob's two-year-old brain became laser-beam focused on inhaling his meal as quickly as possible so he could get to the best part of McDonald's: Playland.

The typical McDonald's Playland comprises two main features: the ball pit and the tubes. While Jacob enjoyed diving into the ball pit as much as the next kid, his true love was the tubes. He loved crawling through the colorful kid-sized tunnels and cruising down the slide at the end. He especially enjoyed climbing up to the very highest spot in the tubes and looking through the clear plastic window. This was his refuge, his happy place. And this is where our story really begins.

On this particular outing, Jacob had been sitting comfortably at the highest spot in the tubes for some time when Lora determined that it was time to head home.

"Jacob, let's go," she called, as she had done on many other occasions. This time, however, Jacob just sat there smiling at her.

Thinking he hadn't heard her, she hoisted her pregnant body up off the hard plastic chair that had been torturing her for the past twenty minutes and moved closer to the tubes. "Jacob, let's go," she called again.

Jacob just smiled and sat there.

Lora looked straight at her son with an expression that clearly said, *Don't you dare mess with a pregnant woman.* "Jacob," she called once more, firmly emphasizing each syllable, "come down here right now!"

Jacob's face showed a growing determination. After he gradually slid back into his happy place, entirely out of view, the ugly reality dawned on Lora: Jacob had no intention of coming down. This had never happened before. Lora mentally sifted through her limited options: Her husband was at work, none of her friends was nearby, and here she was, pregnant as could be.

Anyone who knows Lora knows exactly what she'd do in a situation like this. Without skipping a beat, she slid her shoes off, said, "Excuse me," to a couple of wide-eyed kids, and began to squeeze herself, pregnant body and all, through the colorful winding plastic tubes that housed her son. I wish I could have seen the look of shock on his little face when Lora reached the top of the tubes. I don't think he saw that one coming. Lora promptly escorted him to the exit slide and positioned him between her legs, and they slid down together. The parents who had been watching this escapade greeted them with a round of applause when they reached the bottom. Jacob's reign as Tube King had come to an end.

The next time we went to McDonald's, rather than letting Jacob enjoy some free time, we had him practice coming down from the tubes the *first time* he was called. Once he showed he would listen to his parents in Playland, his privilege of playing there returned.

Why Does Respect Matter?

Like most two-year-olds, Jacob had no idea what the word *respect* meant. However, even at his young age, he was taking his first steps toward learning to be respectful, which in this case meant listening to his mom at McDonald's Playland.

Such lessons are a crucial part of the maturing process for every child because respect is the core of all successful relationships. Whether you're dealing with issues of obedience, sibling arguments, behavior at school, friendship challenges, or any other parenting issue, helping your child make respectful choices lies at the heart of the matter.

However, instead of focusing on respect, we often focus our parenting efforts on teaching our children to be obedient. While obedience is important, respectful behavior goes far beyond obedience, positively shaping our children's responses in a wide variety of situations, such as:

- Responding quickly and politely when Mom or Dad gives instructions or makes a request
- Making comments and asking questions in a thoughtful and self-controlled way
- Expressing feelings without attacking other people or putting them down
- Being flexible when a situation doesn't go as planned

Respect is an important part of family life because each person in a family is important. The Bible tells us that we are handmade by God, who knew all of our days before one of them came to be (see Psalm 139). You, your spouse, and each of your children are of utmost value to God. Each of you is also of utmost value to your family. Just as our bodies have different parts and each part is uniquely important, each person in your family plays a uniquely important role in making your family the close and special family God created it to be.

How do you treat a valuable piece of original artwork? Do you throw it around carelessly, not caring if it gets scuffed or damaged? Not at all. You hold it carefully and place it gently where you know it will be safe from harm. You take measures to protect that item because of its value to you. In other words, you treat it with a great deal of respect.

This is how God wants us to treat one another: as the priceless creations we are. In fact, Jesus said that the greatest two commandments are to "love the Lord your God with all your heart and with all your soul and with all your mind" and to "love your neighbor as yourself" (Matthew 22:37-39). The apostle Peter urges us to "show proper respect to everyone" (1 Peter 2:17). These verses tell us that because we are all God's valuable handiwork, we need to treat our neighbors, and certainly our family members, with value and respect.

But, of course, we can't simply set our loved ones and neighbors on the shelf as we would a piece of artwork. We want to treat them with value and respect during our daily interactions, and we want our children to learn to do the same.

So what does respect actually look like in the course of everyday life? Well, when it comes to your children, respect looks like Megan starting her homework the first time you ask (minus the huffing and puffing). It looks like Trevor sharing and taking turns when he invites friends over to play. It also looks like Emily being flexible when she misses out on a sleepover because of a previous family commitment.

Bottom line: You want your child to learn that being respectful to others in every situation is an important part of obeying God. The problem is that being respectful does not come naturally to most kids. They have to learn how to do it.

Time for a New Approach

In my work as a child psychologist, I have the privilege of meeting all kinds of children, many of whom are wrestling with issues related to respect. One such child was Jimmy, a blond-haired, blue-eyed, freckle-faced ten-year-old whose parents knew they needed to make some changes.

During our first session, when I usually meet with just parents, John and Renee (Jimmy's parents) sat on the overstuffed blue couch in my office and filled me in on the situation.

"What are your main concerns about Jimmy?" I asked, ready to start scribbling on my legal pad.

"Where do I begin?" Renee replied with a note of humor as she rolled her eyes.

"Just tell him what Jimmy does," encouraged John.

"Well, it's more what he doesn't do," Renee said. "He just doesn't listen. When I ask him to do something, he either ignores me or just tells me he's not going to do it. Not all the time, but often enough. And if I call him on it, watch out — it can be World War III. He yells and stomps up the stairs. He even hits his sister if she gets in his way."

"He doesn't always throw fits, but when he does, they're big ones," John added. "Sometimes it's hard to even get him to go to his room for a time-out. It can be a huge battle."

"What do you usually do then?" I asked.

Renee sighed. "We've tried everything. We've shouted, sent him to his room, taken privileges away, and grounded him. I can't think of anything else to take away. Nothing seems to make any difference."

Problem: Their old style of discipline wasn't working.

Solution: They needed a new approach for teaching respectful behavior.

Can you relate to John and Renee's frustration? If so, I have great news for you: It *is* possible to teach our kids to be respectful without resorting to desperate parenting tactics. But first we need to take a fresh look at our parenting approach. What is the best way to raise respectful kids?

Let's answer that question by considering God's divine guidance through the wisest man of his time, perhaps of all time: Solomon. He wrote one of the most significant parenting verses in all of Scripture: "Train a child in the way he should go, and when he is old he will not turn from it" (Proverbs 22:6).

You may notice that Solomon did not tell us to *discipline* our kids in the way they should go. He said to *train* them in the way they should go. This is a very important distinction. The idea of training and teaching our children is woven throughout Scripture. In the first chapter of Proverbs, Solomon commanded, "Listen, my son, to your father's *instruction* and do not forsake your mother's *teaching*" (Proverbs 1:8, emphasis added). Paul picked up the same theme when he advised, "Fathers, do not exasperate your children; instead, bring them up in the *training* and *instruction* of the Lord" (Ephesians 6:4, emphasis added).

Our main role as a parent is that of a trainer, not a disciplinarian. Now, discipline is an important part of training, to be sure, but discipline is only *one part* of training; it's not the whole enchilada. And, like John and Renee, many of us mistakenly focus too much on discipline, relying on negative consequences as our primary parenting tactic rather than teaching and motivating our children to be respectful. This is the biggest strategic mistake we can make. Not only does it take our time and energy away from other valuable training approaches, it also reduces our effectiveness in the long run.

My goal in this book is to help you bring out the best in your child by refocusing your parenting efforts on *training* your child to be respectful. You're already familiar with sports coaches, business coaches, success coaches, and life coaches. Well, we're adding a new one to the list: You're going to become your child's respect coach. *Respectful Kids* will serve as your coach's handbook, complete with everything you need in order to help your child win at the game of respect. In the chapters to follow, you'll learn how to put into action a step-by-step plan for teaching your child to handle any family situation respectfully. This plan incorporates three simple yet extremely effective training strategies to increase your child's respectful behavior while simultaneously decreasing your child's disrespectful behavior. And as you'll see, two-thirds of our efforts will rely on training that takes place *before* the next problem rather than simply reacting to the problem when it happens.

Strategy One: Teach Respectful Behavior

Just as a coach teaches basketball skills to a child, you can teach your child the key skills of respectful behavior. This means you can teach your daughter to put her clothes away the first time you ask. That's worth the price of this book right there. You can show your son how to ask his brother (without ripping his head off) to change the TV channel back. You can even teach your child how to cope with disappointment when someone else gets the last brownie. The key skills covered in the first part of *Respectful Kids* include teaching your kids how to:

- Listen and respond appropriately the first time
- Be flexible and respectful even in the face of disappointment
- Find a solution instead of just arguing about the problem

Like anything worthwhile, respectful behavior isn't learned by osmosis. It requires deliberate, strategic effort. For example, my youngest son, Luke, just finished his first season of competitive fifth-grade basketball. He loved every minute of it, and he and his team had a great season, but they didn't stumble onto success by accident. They experienced a winning season for two main reasons: They had good coaches, and they practiced.

We'll take the same approach with your child. Chances are, one or more of your kids is involved in a sport or activity in which specific skills are developed over time. And no matter how talented your child may be at soccer, T-ball, baseball, basketball, gymnastics, football, hockey, dance, martial arts, music lessons, or whatever his favorite activity, the "P-word" inevitably crops up in his conversations with you and his coach or teacher.

"Practice makes perfect."

"Everyone has to practice."

"The only way to get better is through hard work and practice."

No one doubts the truth of this when it comes to skills such as shooting a basketball or playing the piano, but what does that have to do with being respectful? Well, respect is also a skill, which means it's developed the same way: through practice. Many of us have never thought of respectful behavior that way before.

Here comes the fun part: The more you practice respectful behavior with your child, the more skilled he will become at being respectful. The more skilled he becomes at being respectful in practice, the more easily and naturally he'll draw on those skills in real life. And the more often he uses his new respectful skills in real life, the sooner those skills become a habit.

Do you see how it works? Just as you've seen your child's skills improve at basketball, soccer, or gymnastics, his respectful behavior skills can improve the same way — only without the sweaty shorts.

Strategy Two: Turn On Respectful Behavior

As any good coach knows, a crucial aspect of training is to help your student experience the fun and excitement that comes from mastering a certain skill. A basketball coach wants each of her players to experience the thrill of making a great pass or sinking a game-winning shot. A classroom teacher wants each student to experience the imaginative joy that comes from reading a great book. When a child experiences the natural rewards of an activity, she becomes motivated to continue that activity on her own.

In the same way, you can turn on your child's respectful behavior by helping her experience the positive results that naturally come from it. In the second part of this book, I'll show you how to teach your child that respectful behavior turns on the positives, such as fun privileges and activities, enjoyable interactions with family and friends, and the inner satisfaction of knowing that she is obeying God in the way she treats others. Without bribing or doing anything illegal, you can help your child learn that treating others the way God tells us to is the fastest way to feel great and enjoy many fun privileges.

In short, you want your child to learn that being respectful is fun. No, that was not a misprint. *Fun.* And with a little practice, respectful behavior is really not that difficult. (I've had hundreds of kids actually tell me that.) When your child comes to the conclusion that being respectful is usually pretty easy and is often quite fun or, at the very least, leads to fun — you may want to sit down for this — she will actually *want* to choose respectful behavior. Who wouldn't?

Strategy Three: Turn Off Disrespectful Behavior

Shocking as it may sound, when your child acts disrespectfully, it's probably not an accident. Caught up in the moment, your child believes he has a chance to eke out an extra sixty seconds of TV time if he can stall and argue long enough when you ask him to turn it off. If he didn't think that, he wouldn't do it over and over again. In the privacy of my office, many certified world-class arguers have told me that this is exactly what they think. And as long as your child thinks disrespectful behavior will pay off, you can bet your bottom dollar he'll give it his best shot.

We want to change all this. We want your child to truly believe that disrespectful behavior will never work out in his favor. We want to instill the certainty in his brain that disrespectful behavior will always have three consequences. First, it will work out *bad*, which means it will cancel out privileges and the fun that goes along with them. Second, it will work out bad, *fast*. Third, it will work out bad, fast, *every time*. Those are the three cardinal principles of negative consequences.

The Bible tells us, "No discipline seems pleasant at the time, but painful. Later on, however, it produces a harvest of righteousness and peace for those who have been trained by it" (Hebrews 12:11). Only when your child truly believes that disrespectful behavior will work out bad, fast, every time will he be sufficiently motivated to make the extra effort to be respectful. While being respectful is usually not very difficult, occasionally it can require a little extra work or result in some level of inconvenience. However, this is the nitty-gritty fabric of real life, and God wants your child to learn to handle *every* situation, not just the easy ones, in a way that shows respect and consideration toward others.

In the third part of this book, I'll show you how to turn disrespectful behavior into on-the-spot training opportunities and how to use negative consequences more effectively than ever before to decrease your child's disrespectful behavior. We'll also spend some time learning how to respond to disrespectful behavior the right way — building your child up rather than tearing him down — so that you're building healthy family relationships along the way.

The Big Payoff

As you'll remember, when we first met Jimmy's family, John and Renee were worn out and eager for help. As Renee explained, even a simple request for her son's help around the house could turn ugly in a nanosecond.

> **Renee:** Jimmy, would you please help me empty the dishwasher?
>
> **Jimmy:** No, I did it last time. I'm watching TV.
>
> **Renee:** But Jimmy, your show is over now.
>
> **Jimmy:** There's another one coming on. It's a new episode.
>
> **Renee:** Jimmy, it will take only a minute. Please.
>
> **Jimmy:** No. Make Shannon do it. She never does anything.

There's no doubt about it: Jimmy was trying to get more TV time by arguing his way out of emptying the dishwasher. His disrespectful behavior had paid off enough times — perhaps because Renee was just too tired of arguing — that he had learned it was worth a shot.

But soon after their initial visit to my office, big changes started to unfold in Jimmy's family. Instead of just focusing on discipline, John and Renee centered their efforts on teaching Jimmy to handle everyday situations in a flexible and respectful way. They found fun ways to practice the key skills of respectful behavior together, usually at bedtime, until the new behavior began to feel more natural to Jimmy. I also spent some time practicing with Jimmy and could see these new skills begin to take root.

Using the techniques that you'll learn in this book, John and Renee helped Jimmy see the upside of respectful behavior by turning on the positives that would encourage him to make good choices. Jimmy clearly felt the impact of their efforts. John and Renee also learned how to respond effectively to Jimmy's disrespectful behavior without resorting to shouts and threats. As a result, Jimmy ended up losing several valuable privileges, such as playing his video games and riding his skateboard. There were no fireworks from Mom and Dad—just disrespectful behavior working out bad, fast, every time. As you can imagine, Jimmy wasn't happy about this at all, but it reinforced the reality that only respectful behavior could turn on the positives.

After a few difficult months of up-and-down behavior, Jimmy realized his disrespectful behavior wasn't going to pay off like it had in the past. As John and Renee consistently applied the three key strategies for raising respectful kids, their family relationships and interactions were gradually transformed. Renee told me how delighted she was by one particular conversation:

Renee: Jimmy, would you help me empty the dishwasher?

Jimmy: Do I have to do it right now?

Renee: Yes, that would help me a lot.

Jimmy: (slight pause) Okay, I'm coming.

These results required a lot of work from both Jimmy and his parents, and the transformation didn't happen overnight. It took close to six months for Jimmy's behavior to become consistently more respectful, but as you can imagine, the big payoff was worth it.

The last time I saw Jimmy, he was sitting in my office with a big smile on his face.

Me: Well, Jimmy, how's it going?

Jimmy: Real good.

Me: On a one-to-ten scale, with ten being best, how are

	you doing with being respectful at home?
Jimmy:	About an eight.
Me:	An eight? That's awesome! You've been a seven or
	an eight for a while now. Good for you, pal. Let's
	see what Mom thinks. Mom, how would you rate
	Jimmy's respectful behavior?
Renee:	(with a big smile) I'd have to agree. He's been a
	seven or an eight overall. We have the occasional
	six, but some days are a ten. He's doing great.

As we walked out of my office, Renee pulled me off to the side and told me she felt as if she had her son back. Things were not always perfect in their household, and Jimmy still had a bad day now and then (who doesn't?), but John and Renee felt much more confident in their ability to respond to negative behavior when it popped up.

Ready for a Change?

I'm sure both John and Renee would tell you that if Jimmy could learn to be respectful, your child can too. Yes, some kids are more strong-willed than others, and for them the learning process may take a little longer.[1] But whatever your child's temperament, the strategies in *Respectful Kids* will propel you and your child down the path toward having a more respectful family.

Are you ready to teach your child how to respond to life's challenges in a respectful way? Are you ready to trade your child's bad habits in for good ones? Are you ready for a more respectful family? Then let me show you how to turn on the respectful behavior and bring out the best in your child.

- Respectful behavior lies at the heart of successful relationships.
- Respect is a crucial part of your family life because every person in your family is important.
- Being respectful does not come naturally to most kids. They have to learn how to do it.
- You can teach your child the key skills of respectful behavior.
- Transformation won't happen overnight, but the big payoff is worth the investment.

TAKING THE NEXT STEP

1. Read Proverbs 1:8-9, Proverbs 22:6, and Ephesians 6:4. Write out your "Top 5" list of lessons you want to teach your child.

2. Read Matthew 22:37-39 and Luke 6:31. How do you define respect in your family?

3. Name an area of life — such as academics, sports, or music — in which your child has benefited from practice. What do you think might change if you regularly help him practice respectful behavior?

4. What do you think about the idea of teaching your kids that respectful behavior leads to fun? List a few natural benefits of respectful behavior.

5. How do you feel when someone makes a positive remark about your respectful behavior? What impact does that encouragement have on you?

6. List the three main discipline approaches you usually rely on. Rate their effectiveness on a scale of 1 to 10, with 10 being the most effective. Explain why you think each approach is effective or ineffective.

7. Describe a recent scenario in which your child responded disrespectfully. Now describe how you'd like to see that same scenario play out in the future.

8. Honesty time: If your discipline efforts were videotaped for an entire week, what percentage of them would you not want to be aired on the next *Oprah* show? Explain your answer.

1

Teach Respectful Behavior

A family is where a child learns to display affection, control his temper, and pick up his toys.

MARIANNE E. NEIFERT

I will instruct you and teach you in the way you should go.

PSALM 32

CHAPTER 2

A Quick Look in the Bathroom Mirror

guess who's watching when you're not looking?

O ne summer afternoon several years ago, I was slaving away at one of my least favorite household chores: mowing the lawn. The kids were outside enjoying the warm, sunny day, shooting baskets and climbing through the nooks and crannies of our multicolored jungle gym. I was half-finished mowing the front lawn, walking back and forth parallel with the sidewalk, when out of the corner of my eye I caught a glimpse of something moving.

On the sidewalk, my four-year-old son, Luke, was keeping perfect pace with me as he pushed his plastic toy lawnmower (the kind that shoots bubbles out of the top) with all the seriousness and determination of a professional landscaper. He was doing exactly what he saw his dad doing.

As I continued to mow, so did he. When I walked, he walked. When I turned, he turned. Where's the video camera when you need it? After a couple minutes of this, I was so tickled that I stopped the lawnmower, walked over to Luke, gave him a high five, and congratulated him on doing such a great job of mowing the sidewalk. But deep inside, a more serious thought gripped my heart: *If Luke is imitating me on something as insignificant as mowing the lawn, how much more closely will he imitate me in things that really do matter?*

I'll be honest with you: That thought bothered me. It actually scared me a little, and I had a hard time shaking it from my mind over the next few days. My mind kept racing through a list of my personal sins, my areas of struggle. Would my sons observe me taking a second look at a bikini-clad model on a TV commercial? Would they catch me raising my voice in anger when they disobeyed? Would they notice that I haven't read my Bible much in the past week?

Parent Habits Lead to Child Habits

My son's innocent imitation reminded me that all the lessons we as parents want to teach our children begin in the same place: our example.

When it comes to the issue of respect — as well as other family concerns — before we can improve our child's habits, we have to take a look at our own. Webster's dictionary defines *habit* as "an acquired mode of behavior that has become nearly or completely involuntary."[2] It's something we have done so often that we begin to do it automatically. And those automatic behaviors influence both our present and our future. More than two thousand years ago, Aristotle observed, "We are what we repeatedly do. Excellence, then, is not an act, but a habit."[3]

Your child is developing habits as you sit and read this book. The ways he talks and acts every day are slowly becoming part of his automatic behavior. Those habits impact every aspect of family life, from how he reacts when you ask him to pick up his socks to what he does when his sister makes the mistake of breathing in his airspace.

It should come as no surprise that God wants our kids to develop good habits because he has their best interests in mind. The surprise is that he intends to accomplish this through people like you and me.

Consider this: Your child sees you in the morning before your first cup of coffee. That's scary enough right there. She sees you when the laundry is all caught up and the world is good. She sees you when you're angry with your spouse, your computer crashes, and the cat throws up. She sees how you really are — not how you say you are or how you wish you were. Your child has a more accurate picture of you than many of your friends do. She sees the real thing, every day.

And what she sees impacts her behavior. Why? Because your child will see and experience your habits thousands of times. And with that much repetition, something is bound to rub off. For instance, if your volume level usually sounds like you have a megaphone strapped to your head, your child will conclude that shouting is okay and adopt that behavior for himself. A mother of a three-year-old boy recently told me, "I know where he gets his shouting from — me." If you tend to be chronically late, your child may decide that getting ready for school on time isn't all that important. If you never change the toilet paper roll . . . well, you get the idea.

If your child is disobeying, arguing, throwing anger fits, or talking disrespectfully, chances are, these are simply bad habits he has developed.

Bad news: His bad habits may be a reflection of your habits.

Good news: Bad habits can be replaced with good ones.

A Picture of Respect

If you've completed a few jigsaw puzzles in your time, then you know the routine. First you spread out all the pieces on a table. Then you turn them right side up. Next you find the corners and edges and make your border. Those are the easy parts.

Once you've finished the border, the real work of completing the puzzle begins. This is when you realize you are utterly dependent on one irreplaceable object: the picture on the box cover. Complete chaos can break out if several people are working on the puzzle with only one picture to share among them. Everyone needs the picture in order to complete their portion of the puzzle — and they need it now!

Why is the box cover so essential? Because it's virtually impossible to complete the puzzle without it! Most people need to see the picture on the box cover and study it in painstaking detail to determine which piece they need to find next or what to do with the odd-shaped piece they've picked up. In fact, progress can come to a dead stop until you get your hands on that picture.

Mom, Dad, you are the picture God has placed in your children's lives. You are the picture on the box top that they can't do without. You are the picture they are studying for clues, just as if they were completing a jigsaw puzzle. But they're attempting something far more difficult and significant: They're trying to become young men and women who love and follow God in a world that will put their faith and commitment to the test. They're trying to learn what it means to be authentic followers of Christ.

Knowing the challenges they will face and their need for a concrete example to follow, God has given them a picture to look at: you! And looking at you is meant to lead them to him. Yes, they will look at the example of Jesus in Scripture to get a glimpse of what God is like and how he wants to transform them into his image. But you are the real-life picture in the here and now. You are the picture they can see and touch and talk to. You are the picture that God has strategically placed in their lives to point them to himself.

Like it or not, your children's eyes are on you. And what they see and hear will influence their present and their eternity. So when your children look at you, what kind of picture are they looking at?

- A picture of compassion and understanding, or of unreasonable expectations?
- A picture of unshakeable honesty, or of shading the truth when it's more convenient?
- A picture of taking personal responsibility, or of making excuses?
- A picture that encourages others, or that tears them down?

- A picture of self-control, or of abusive anger?
- A picture that can be flexible, or that becomes unyielding?

If you're feeling a bit of regret over your less-than-ideal parental portrait, I want to remind you that none of us always gives our children a perfect picture. Heaven knows I don't. In fact, a perfect picture won't do our kids any good, because they won't be able to relate to it or ever duplicate it.

Our children don't need a perfect picture; they need an authentic picture — the real thing. Knowing the eternal impact of our assignment, we try our best to get things right. But when we fail — as we all inevitably do — our children need to see us get up off the ground, brush ourselves off, apologize to whomever we have hurt, and then get back to the business of following God. Why do our kids need to see this? Because they'll need to do it countless times themselves as they make mistakes along the way.

God did not just put your child in your life; he also purposely placed you in hers. Let that sink in for a minute. God put you in your child's life for a purpose. You have many jobs as a parent, but one of the most important is to be the picture that God placed you in your family to be. The most effective tool you have for raising respectful kids is to be a respectful parent.

Sharpening the Image

So how can we be the pictures God intends us to be? How can we give our children the clearest view of what it looks like to be respectful to others as we genuinely follow God?

First, *we identify those aspects of our behavior that need to change.* These may include, but not be limited to, the following areas:

- How we talk to our spouse
- The amount of time we spend with our kids

- How we express frustration
- The tone and volume of our voice when we correct our children
- The way we work through family problems
- The reasonableness of our expectations in relation to the age and understanding of our children
- How we joke with our kids
- The consistency of our devotional times

When we admit that something needs to change, we open the door for God to begin working in that area. It seems I'm always finding an issue that needs fine-tuning. The most recent examples that come to mind are my tendency to become overfocused on my work and my inconsistency with my devotional times. One mom shared with me her tendency to expect too much from her kids, forgetting that her children are not mini-adults but have lesser thresholds of hunger and tiredness and can't always keep up with a busy adult schedule.

Second, *we surrender that area to God.* The harder we try to change on our own, the more we tend to make a mess of things. The Bible tells us that God will never turn away a broken and contrite heart (see Psalm 51:17), which is something I often find myself dealing with as I consider my many imperfections. It's good to know that God is more than able to complete the good work he has begun in us if we humbly admit our faults and come to him for help (see James 4:10; Philippians 1:6; 1 John 1:8-9).

Third, *we take it out of the closet.* This doesn't mean we have to confess our sins to the entire church congregation next Sunday (whew!), but it does involve finding a trusted person to confide in and share our struggles with. This may be your spouse, a close friend, an accountability group or partner, your pastor, or a counselor. My wife, Lora, has been a great sounding board and adviser for me on many issues (and her rates are reasonable). At other times, I've been blessed with several great guy friends with whom I've been able to share my personal struggles. Talking with someone about our problems gets the issues out in the open, where healing and change can begin.

Fourth, *we get specific about how to move toward change.* What changes do we need to make in our schedule, or the words we use, or the actions we choose? Together with our trusted person, we can identify specific steps that will help us begin to make changes in the picture we present to our children every day. Here are a few action steps that I, or other parents I've known, have taken to address issues we wanted to focus on:

- Make a list of hurtful words you will no longer use.
- Commit yourself to apologizing to your child every time you lose your temper with her.
- Limit Internet and TV time to free up more time to be with your family.
- Say one positive thing to each child every day.
- Compliment your spouse in front of your kids.
- Physically touch each child in a caring, appropriate way every day.
- Spend a couple minutes at each bedtime asking your child about her day.
- Take each child out to breakfast once a month.
- Lead a short family devotion each morning.
- Prepare a family-time discussion once a week.
- Read five chapters from the Bible each week.
- Have a date night with your spouse once a month.
- Pray with your spouse each night before going to bed.
- Make an appointment with a marriage or family counselor.

We can let our trusted friend know which action steps we will take and ask him or her to check with us to see if we've followed through. There's nothing like a little accountability to help us get moving in the right direction.

Through these four steps, God can begin to shape our lives into the picture our children need to look at every day. While none of us is perfect, we can find encouragement and experience lasting change by surrendering our lives to God and taking steps to obey him in each area of our family relationships.

As we allow God to develop us into the picture he created us to be, our children will find it easier to become everything he made them to be.

- Parent habits influence child habits.
- You are the picture God has placed in your child's life.
- Your child doesn't need a perfect picture; he needs an authentic picture.
- When we admit that something needs to change, we open the door for God to begin working.
- God can shape your life into the picture your child needs to see every day.

TAKING THE NEXT STEP

1. Read Deuteronomy 6:4-9 and 1 Corinthians 11:1. What do these verses suggest about how your example influences your child? Why is your example so important?

2. How would you describe your child's view of God? How much of that came from you?

3. As you look back on your childhood, what impact did your parents' example have on your life?

4. Describe a behavior — positive or negative — that your child most likely has picked up from you.

5. Brownie point time: If you're married, name two of your spouse's habits that you appreciate. Now name one of your own good habits. How do these habits positively affect your family?

6. Here comes the tough part: Name one of your own bad habits. If left unchecked, what impact will this habit have on your life? What impact will it have on your child's perspective or life?

7. If God purposely placed you in your child's life, what is one of your unique, God-given characteristics or traits that can positively influence that child's life?

8. List one change you think God wants you to make in your "box-top picture." What specific steps can you take to make that change happen? Who will you ask to hold you accountable for taking these steps?

CHAPTER 3

Just Say "Okay" and Do It!

the skill of fast listening

L ike any good coach, you need to start with the fundamentals. Fast listening is the respect skill equivalent to learning to dribble a basketball with one hand for the first-grade basketball player or memorizing the names of the notes on the piano for the first-time piano student. Because fast listening is a relatively simple skill that's called for daily, it's the perfect place to begin.

Ideally, when you ask your child to pick up her toys from the family room floor, what do you want her to do?

a. Argue
b. Ignore you
c. Throw a fit
d. Say, "Okay, Mom, I'd be happy to. And while I'm at it, perhaps I can help you put away the dishes."

Well, perhaps we're taking things a bit far with answer D, but I'm willing to wager that it's your top choice.

When I ask my boys to do something, I'd like them to say, "Sure,

Dad," and do it. Perhaps they can ask a question in a respectful way, if they have one. Or they can make a respectful comment, if the setting is appropriate. That doesn't seem too difficult. Yet every day thousands of children and teenagers fail to respond this way when their parents make a request. Why? It's not as if parents fail to express their expectations. The kids have heard it a thousand times: "You need to be respectful, young man!" They've been lectured until their ears hurt. But they've never really been taught the skills they need to be respectful.

So let's take a look at the first skill for developing world-class respectful behavior: fast listening.

Fast Listening: The Basics

Do you remember Jimmy from chapter 1? When he first visited my office, Jimmy was what I call a slow listener. This means that when his parents asked Jimmy to do something, he typically responded by ignoring, arguing, whining, complaining, talking back, and, of course, not doing the thing he was asked to do. Needless to say, Jimmy's slow listening wasn't working out well for him or his family. Jimmy needed to develop the skill of fast listening.

Fast listening refers to an appropriate response to a parental request. In other words, it's a shorthand term for how you want your child to respond when you ask her to do something: You want her to obey promptly and communicate respectfully, an expectation founded on biblical principles. The apostle Paul wrote, "Children, obey your parents in the Lord, for this is right" (Ephesians 6:1). He also encouraged us to "do everything without complaining or arguing" (Philippians 2:14). Obeying parents and communicating respectfully are two valuable lessons your child needs to learn, and they are the essence of fast listening.

Fast listening is really quite simple. It involves something for your child to *say* and something for him to *do*. When you ask your child to do something, you want him to *say*, "Okay, Mom/Dad," or ask a question in a respectful way, and then *do* it (do exactly what you've asked).

In most cases, fast listening simply means that your child will verbally agree to what you've asked and then do it. However, at times your child can respond with an appropriate question. For example, if you ask Brandon to turn off the TV but the show he's watching still has a few minutes left, it's reasonable for him to ask if he can watch the last few minutes of the show. The critical issue is not *if* he asks but *how* he asks. We don't want any arguing, whining, complaining, or disrespect. We want him to ask his question in a respectful manner: "Hey, Mom, can I just watch the last few minutes of this program?" This isn't arguing; it's respectfully asking a question — and it's a perfectly reasonable part of fast listening. We're not trying to raise robots; we're trying to raise intelligent, reasoning children who understand the art of respectful communication. If you tell Brandon he's allowed to watch a few extra minutes, then great. If not, then you want him to be flexible and turn off the TV right away. (We'll look at the skill of flexible thinking in the next chapter.)

Fast listening can be applied to any situation in which you ask your child to do something, such as completing his homework, getting ready for bed, and coming in from playing outside. And with just a little practice, any child can master this skill.

Helping Your Child Master the Skill of Fast Listening

Just as a basketball coach doesn't send a rookie out onto the court and expect him to perform with the excellence of an All-Star player, we can't expect our children to demonstrate fast listening in real life without first having some practice. That's where *you* come in. Fast listening practice is about to begin.

Getting Started

Fast listening practice can be fun and accomplished in a relatively short amount of time. It's best to introduce the concept of fast listening to your child during a neutral time — in other words, not while you're frustrated or angry about her behavior. When I introduce fast listening to a child, I cover four main points:

1. There are two types of listening: fast listening and slow listening.
2. Slow listening brings negative consequences, such as time-out, loss of privileges, and arguments.
3. Fast listening brings positive results, such as closer relationships, pleasing God, less fighting, and more privileges.
4. Fast listening is easy; it requires only two steps.

Here's how I introduced fast listening during my second session with eleven-year-old Haley, whose finely tuned arguing skills were second to none:

Me:	Haley, which do you like more, having fun or feeling sad and mad?
Haley:	Having fun.
Me:	Great. Me too. Then you'll love the thing we're going to learn today, because it will help your fun to shoot through the roof. Does that sound all right?
Haley:	Yeah, sure.
Me:	Okay, it's called fast listening. When your mom and dad ask you to do something, you can do one of two things: slow listening or fast listening. Slow listening is when you ignore your mom and dad, argue, complain, talk back, and don't do what they ask you to do. Have you ever used slow listening before?
Haley:	(with a grin) Yeah, sometimes.
Me:	How does it usually work out when you use slow listening?

Haley:	Not too good.
Me:	That sounds about right. Slow listening usually gets kids in trouble. They get sent to time-out or lose privileges, their parents get angry — it generally works out bad. But fast listening works out awesome. It makes for more fun, you don't get in trouble, and you get along better with your parents. It's also a great way to obey God, because you'll be treating your parents respectfully when they ask you to do something. Sounds pretty good, huh?
Haley:	Yeah.

At this point, Haley understands that she has two options when faced with a parental request: slow listening and fast listening. I've emphasized the huge difference in outcome that each brings, using simple language she can easily understand. She is now starting to get curious about this new skill that brings such great results.

Me:	And, Haley, check this out. Fast listening is actually quite easy. Fast listening has two parts: something to *say* and something to *do*. Let's start with the "say" part. When your mom or dad asks you to do something, there are two words that will become your new best friends. Can you guess what they are?
Haley:	No clue.
Me:	Then get ready, here they come — (anticipatory pause) — "Okay, Mom" or "Okay, Dad." Say that with me.
Haley:	"Okay, Mom" or "Okay, Dad."
Me:	Beautiful. Those words sound *really* respectful, don't they? That's why they work so well. Now,

"Okay, Mom" or "Okay, Dad" is what you'd say most of the time, because most of the stuff your parents ask you to do is pretty simple and you might as well just go ahead and do it. However, sometimes you may have a question about something your parents ask you to do — like if they tell you to turn off the TV but your show isn't over yet. In that case, it's perfectly fine to ask a question — as long as you do it in a respectful way. Does that make sense?

Haley: Yeah, that makes sense.

Me: Show me how you'd ask your mom in a respectful way if you could finish your TV program.

Haley: Mom, can I finish watching my show? It's not over yet.

Me: You've got the idea. So when your parents ask you to do something, you can say, "Okay, Mom" or "Okay, Dad," or you can ask a question in a respectful way. How does that sound so far?

Haley: That sounds all right.

Me: Now, there's only one more part to fast listening: the "do" part. After you've said, "Okay, Mom" or "Okay, Dad," what action should you take?

Haley: Just do what they asked?

Me: Perfect. You should just do it. And should you do it slow or fast?

Haley: Fast?

Me: Right again. You should do it fast, because you're fast listening. If you did it slow, you'd be slow listening, and we know that always works out bad. So what two words do you say to show that you are practicing fast listening?

Haley: "Okay, Mom" or "Okay, Dad."

Me:	And if you need to ask a question, you ask it in a . . .
Haley:	Respectful way.
Me:	You're a fast learner. And then what do you do? You just . . .
Haley:	Do it.
Me:	You've got it.

Practicing for Real-Life Success

Once you've introduced the concept of fast listening to your child, your next goal is to help him make it a regular habit. This simply takes a bit of practice. Just as your child won't play basketball like Michael Jordan after one practice or become Mozart after one piano lesson, he won't build respectful habits without practice either.

I've learned that two simple practice components — *memorization* and *application* — will help your child learn to use fast listening as quickly as possible:

Memorization. In order for your child to apply fast listening to everyday situations, she needs to memorize the fast-listening steps. It will be hard for her to apply fast listening if she doesn't even remember what it is. I usually have a child repeat the fast listening steps after me a few times, as I did with Haley, and then quiz her until she can easily say them from memory. Most children can complete their memorization in just a few minutes, but until fast listening becomes ingrained as a habit for your child, you'll want to quiz her periodically to make sure that the steps — *say* and *do* — remain fresh in her memory.

Application. This component involves helping your child grasp how to follow those steps in real life. Using a common family scenario or a recent slow-listening situation, you'll role play with your child, prompting her to show you how she would put her fast-listening skill to work. Again, pick a neutral time for your practice. If your child's already in trouble for slow listening or your emotions are running high, a training session may only lead to greater trouble. Instead watch for times when the two of you are feeling relaxed and comfortable together. You can practice at bedtime, while having a snack, or whenever it's convenient for you. Here are some scenarios you might want to practice together:

- Putting toys away
- Getting ready for bed
- Starting homework
- Cleaning her room
- Helping with the dishes
- Coming in from playing outside
- Turning off a video game

For example, if your child argued about getting ready for bed last night, you can practice how she could have used fast listening instead. Here's how I practiced this scenario with Haley:

Me: Ready for a fast listening quiz?

Haley: I guess so.

Me: What two words do you say to show that you are fast listening?

Haley: "Okay, Mom" or "Okay, Dad."

Me: Great. And if you need to ask a question, how would you ask it?

Haley: In a polite way or a respectful way.

Me: You've got this down. Now, after you say "Okay, Mom," what action do you take?

Haley: Just do it.

Me: Very nice. Now let's pretend it's a school night and your mom just asked you to get ready for bed. Show me how you would use fast listening. I'll be Mom. Ready?

Haley: Okay.

Me: (pretending to be Mom) Haley, it's time for bed.

	Please turn off the TV and get your pajamas on.
Haley:	I'd say, "Okay, Mom," and get ready for bed.
Me:	That's awesome. You're making this sound too easy. Let's make it a little harder. Let's pretend that you're really not tired and you'd like to stay up a little longer. How would you ask a question about that in a respectful way?
Haley:	(in a whiny tone) Mom, I don't want to go to bed.
Me:	Was that a question or a statement?
Haley:	A statement, I guess.
Me:	Right, it was. The key is to ask a *question* and to ask it in a respectful way — which means using a friendly voice. Give it another try.
Haley:	Mom, I'm not very tired. Can I stay up a bit longer?
Me:	That sounded very respectful. Good job. Now tell me what you would say if Mom answered like this: "Well, Haley, it's a school night and you have to get up early in the morning. You can stay up later on the weekend, so please get your pajamas on and brush your teeth."
Haley:	Okay, Mom.
Me:	And what would you do?
Haley:	Go upstairs and get ready for bed.
Me:	You didn't get the answer from Mom that you were hoping for, but you still used fast listening. How do you think that would work out for you?
Haley:	It would work out fine. I'd just go to bed. I do have to get up early in the morning and I'm probably tired anyway. It's not worth fighting about. I can stay up later on the weekend.
Me:	So you think fast listening would work out better than slow listening?

Haley:	Yeah, I do.
Me:	Me too.

Keeping the practices short will help hold your child's attention and interest, so I strongly recommend keeping them between two to three minutes long. Look for ways to make your practice sessions fun and encouraging. Since you're trying to reinforce the message that respectful behavior leads to fun, you don't want this to feel like hard work.

If your child makes a mistake, remind her of the steps and let her try again. Remember, as her respect coach, you're helping her perfect her skills in this one-on-one lesson so she'll be ready to put them to work in real life. Sometimes, just for fun, I'll role play what slow listening would look like in a certain situation and then contrast that with what fast listening would look like. It's also important to make sure your child understands that asking a question in a respectful way means to use respectful words and a calm, friendly voice. Respectful communication is a key part of every skill we're going to cover in this book.

I suggest practicing daily at first, trying out the steps in various scenarios, and then decreasing the frequency of your sessions as your child displays fast listening more often in daily life. And like any coach who knows how to really motivate a child, you'll want to be sure to fill your practices with plenty of positive, encouraging comments, such as, "Haley, you're doing such a great job of learning to use fast listening. Good for you!"

On-the-Spot Training

After you've introduced your child to the basics of fast listening and put him through a few fast-listening drills, a wonderful opportunity opens up for you in real-life situations. You can begin to do on-the-spot training with your child, just as you would when coaching a child during the heat of a real basketball game. For example, when Nathan starts to argue, you can help him resist the pull of old habits by giving him a verbal cue or reminder:

- "Nathan, this is a time for fast listening, pal."
- "Nathan, are you using fast listening?"
- "You can choose fast listening or slow listening, Nathan. It's up to you."

You can also give this reminder *while* you make your request. For example, you might say, "Nathan, please put your towel in the laundry basket. And remember, fast listening, please. Thanks, buddy."

Here's where your consistent practice really pays off. Your cues will immediately bring all those fun rehearsals back to Nathan's mind, and he will remember that fast listening is pretty easy and works out light years better than slow listening. The fact that he has practiced fast listening many times (and enjoyed it) will greatly increase the odds of his turning things around when you cue him.

Remember your role as your child's respect coach. If he chooses slow listening, which will happen occasionally, use that situation as the focal point of your next practice. Review the situation as it happened, and then ask him a question that helps him see for himself that fast listening offers a much better solution:

- How could you have used fast listening in that situation?
- If you needed to ask a question, how could you have asked it in a respectful way?
- How well did slow listening (arguing, throwing a fit) work?
- What would have happened if you had used fast listening?
- The next time this situation happens, how would you like to handle it?

Then run through the appropriate fast-listening steps in your practice session, just as you've done before, but this time using the recent real-life scenario to reinforce the lesson that fast listening is always the best choice.

Coping with a Reluctant Student

Although most kids are quickly engaged by the enjoyable practice sessions, over the years I've run into a few kids who refuse to practice fast listening with their parents, at least initially. If your child resists the idea, I have a few suggestions that may help.

First, I recommend that you encourage your child to practice fast listening, but don't force the issue. After all, you really can't *make* your child practice. Attempting to coerce her just creates a battle of wills — one you're likely to lose. If you calmly respect her choice rather than creating a power struggle, you'll make it easier for her to change her mind later on.

Second, gently remind your child of the fact that slow listening always works out bad. Tell her that just as fast listening will increase her privileges and family fun, slow listening will decrease them. Let her know that because you love her, you just want to help her avoid the negative consequences that come from slow listening.

Third, periodically remind your child that you'd be happy to help her practice fast listening if she's interested, but it's up to her. You can bring up a recent slow-listening situation and ask how she thinks it worked out. You might ask her one of the review questions suggested earlier to see if she'll talk about it. In the meantime, continue to apply the rest of the strategies in this book. Your child will soon experience the reality that slow listening turns off her privileges and that fast listening is the only way to turn them back on. As you stick with the program, she'll eventually realize that a few minutes of fast-listening practice may not be such a bad idea after all.

You Get Out What You Put In

Let's say I have a bubblegum machine that's half-filled with only yellow gumballs. If I put a quarter into this bubblegum machine, what color of gumball will I get out? The answer, of course, is yellow. If yellow is all that's in there, then yellow is all that's coming out.

But what would happen if I unscrewed the lid and began dropping red gumballs in? Pretty soon there would be as many red gumballs as yellow. Now what happens when I put a quarter in? I'll start getting some red gumballs as well as yellow gumballs. And if I keep putting in red gumballs, I'll soon be getting far more red gumballs than yellow. Why? Because the more red gumballs I put in, the more are available to come rolling out.

Now picture your child's head as that bubblegum machine. Each yellow gumball represents one of your child's bad habits, such as arguing or talking back. Each red gumball, by contrast, represents one fast-listening practice. The more often you practice fast listening with your child, the more those practices take hold and begin to overpower the bad habits that he had previously developed.

As you continue to practice fast listening in a fun way week after week, all that repetition begins to permeate your child's thinking. He'll begin to realize that respectful behavior isn't that difficult after all and that, in fact, it can often be downright fun. God designed it that way. Over time your child will begin to use fast listening in real life without even thinking about it. Fast listening will gradually become more automatic, and slow listening will become less and less natural. In the same way that the red gumballs begin to outnumber the yellow, fast listening skills will begin to roll out through your child's words and actions.

If this sounds like parenting paradise, then break out the sunscreen and pull up a beach chair. We're just getting warmed up. In the next few chapters, we'll be expanding your child's range of respect skills, bringing even more opportunities for your family to bask in the warmth of respectful behavior.

- Obeying parents and communicating respectfully are the essence of fast listening.
- Fast listening can be applied to any situation in which you make a request of your child.
- Two practice components — memorization and application — will help your child learn to use fast listening as quickly as possible.
- You can help your child resist the pull of old habits by giving a verbal cue or reminder for fast listening.
- As you continue to review and practice fast listening together, your child will start to use fast listening without even thinking about it.

1. Read Ephesians 6:1-3, Philippians 2:14-15, and Proverbs 13:3. Why is it so important for your child to learn to listen to her parents and ask questions in a respectful way?

2. You are your child's respect coach. List three characteristics of a good coach, and describe how these characteristics will make your fast listening practices effective.

3. Name two scenarios — such as brushing teeth, doing homework, putting away toys, coming in from playing outside — you'd like to role play to help your child practice fast listening. Why did you choose those situations?

4. If you practice fast listening several times a week with your child, what impact do you think it will have on her behavior in a week? In a month?

5. How do you think your child will respond to fast-listening practice? How can you make the practice sessions fun and enjoyable?

6. Just as a coach calls out plays and reminders during a game, you can cue your child when she uses slow listening. How can you make your on-the-spot training as effective as possible?

7. Describe the changes you hope to see — in your child, in your family, in your daily routine — once your child becomes proficient at fast listening.

8. Consider trying your hand at introducing and teaching fast listening with your spouse or a parent friend before you try it with your child. One of you can pretend to be a child while the other introduces and teaches fast listening, and then switch roles.

CHAPTER 4

It's No Big Deal

the skill of flexible thinking

" He shoots! Oh, what a save!"

That was me, lunging across the floor and screaming out the play-by-play as my elementary-aged sons and I worked ourselves into a sweaty mess playing carpet hockey in the basement. Our equipment was somewhat less than NHL standard. My boys each had oversized plastic hockey sticks, and I used a plastic caveman club for a goalie stick. Our puck was a soft sponge ball. The goal was the basement couch. As the goalie, I was secretly pretending to be Ken Dryden of the Montreal Canadiens, one of my childhood hockey heroes. When either of my boys dared to score, the fun really began. Suddenly transformed into the dreaded tickle goalie, I'd throw down my stick/club and race after them. Eyes open wide with excitement, they'd shriek with joy and sprint off to escape my ticklish wrath.

We'd stay in the basement for hours, enjoying the hockey, the tickling, and the bonding that naturally resulted. Lora would walk downstairs, take one whiff of her sweaty men, and promptly turn around to seek the nearest air freshener.

Then one day I noticed that arguing and complaining had crept into the room, pushing out some of our hockey game fun. Was that really a goal, or did it hit the post? Who had the highest score? Someone got hit in the leg with a hockey stick — was it on purpose or an accident? Our bonding time had become bickering time.

As I reflected on this, I realized that these were normal frustrations that any boys would experience during this type of play. In fact, I experienced the very same situations that my boys did. Sometimes my shots missed the goal and hit the post. I occasionally got whacked with a hockey stick. But I wasn't going ballistic over it. Why? What was I doing that they had not yet learned to do?

It's All in Your Head

I quickly realized the answer. Though all three of us experienced the same events during our hockey game, our resulting feelings and responses were quite different. One boy shot the puck but missed the couch/goal and ended up feeling angry and acting angry. I, too, shot and missed the couch, but I ended up feeling okay about it and still had a good time. It was almost like two different equations:

Miss a goal + _____ = respond with anger and frustration
Miss a goal + _____ = respond with calm and respect

The difference in the outcome clearly came from the second ingredient in each equation. What was that ingredient? *A style of thinking.* It wasn't the fact that someone missed a goal that determined the outcome; it was *how he thought about it* that made all the difference:

Miss a goal + <u>mad thoughts</u> = respond with anger and frustration
Miss a goal + <u>flexible thoughts</u> = respond with calm and respect

My boys were reflexively thinking mad thoughts and then reacting with anger and resentment when things didn't go their way. By contrast, my flexible thinking — emphasizing the positives and quickly releasing any disappointment — allowed me to respond calmly and respectfully in the same situations.

For some kids — and some adults — mad thoughts come to mind with little effort. All of us have had our share of mad thoughts on occasion. Here are a few classics from the Mad Thought Hall of Fame:

That's not fair!
He cheated!
You're so mean!
He did that on purpose!
I lose at everything!
I never get to do anything fun!
All my friends' parents are nicer than you!

Ever heard any of those lines from your child? Do you remember thinking them yourself as a kid? Of course, it's natural for any of us to feel some negative emotions when things don't go our way. But emotions are the result of a thought process, much of which happens so quickly that we may not even be aware of it. When we cultivate the habit of responding to situations with mad thoughts, those thoughts create angry feelings, which can lead to disrespectful behavior.

I saw this happen before my very eyes when my boys got caught up in their mad thoughts and our fun family activity got swept into the penalty box. To reclaim the former joy of our basement hockey games, my boys needed to learn to adopt flexible thinking that would help them honor God and treat each other respectfully. They needed to be "made new in the attitude of [their] minds" (Ephesians 4:23), and it was my job as their coach to show them how.

So we sat down one afternoon and talked about how to bring the fun back to our hockey games. We made a list of things we could say to ourselves in our heads that would honor God and help us stay calm and friendly — even if we got whacked on the leg. Here are some of the flexible thoughts we came up with to replace the mad thoughts that were ruining our hockey games:

I'm having fun with my family.
I can have fun even if I lose.
He made a nice shot.
If I keep trying, I'll get a goal.
I'm thankful for the family God gave me.
No one wins all the time.
He probably didn't mean to push me.

Each thought on our list was balanced, reasonable, and geared to remind us to treat others the way we'd like to be treated (see Matthew 7:12). We talked about how we would all use these thoughts at different points in our hockey games. Then I decided to try something a little crazy.

I started thinking out loud.

Thinking Out Loud

As we discussed in chapter 2, the most effective tool we have as parents is our own example. Social science studies have repeatedly shown that kids tend to imitate what they see and hear, whether watching TV or observing their parents at the dining room table. The apostle Paul clearly understood the power of modeling Christlike behavior; he encouraged the Corinthian believers to follow his example as he followed the example of Christ (see 1 Corinthians 11:1).

As I considered how I might teach my boys to be flexible and cope with the unpredictable circumstances of a basement hockey game, I figured Jesus would be the master of flexible thoughts and good sportsmanship if he were playing with us. (Whether Jesus would be playing hockey at all is a question I'll leave to the theologians.) I reasoned that if I copied him, maybe my boys would copy me. After all, I'm one of the pictures God gave them to show what it means to follow him in every area of life, including basement hockey games (Lora being the other picture, of course).

Then an even more powerful idea dawned on me: Instead of keeping all of my flexible thoughts to myself, I could think them out loud so my boys could hear them. By thinking out loud, I could give them a real-life picture of how to stay calm, flexible, and friendly during our hockey game. They would hear the exact thoughts old Dad was using when they scored on me or when I got whacked on the leg.

The next time we played basement hockey, I was ready. As we moved into our positions to play, before the first shot was even taken, I looked at Luke and Jacob and said, "I'm sure glad to be playing with you guys. I don't even care who wins. It's fun either way." A few minutes later, when Jacob shot the sponge ball and it wasn't clear whether he had scored or not, I took advantage of the situation and calmly remarked, "We'll count it as a goal. It's no big deal. Good shot, buddy."

Throughout the game, I continually verbalized flexible thoughts. Sometimes I complimented the boys; other times I simply made positive observations. I frequently expressed how much I enjoyed playing with them. I voiced flexible ways of thinking about any situation that came up. All of these were things I was usually thinking anyway; it's just that now I was thinking them out loud so my boys could learn from them.

Within the next two or three hockey matches, I began to notice a gradual shift in the emotional climate. The cloud that had settled over our hockey games was beginning to lift. We still had the occasional feather ruffling, but it was less frequent and more easily turned around. But here's the kicker: I started to notice my boys using the same flexible expressions that I'd been modeling:

"That's okay. It's just a game."
"I went first last time. You can go first this time."
"Even though I lost, I still had fun."

Bingo. Chalk one up for the old man.

Once I saw that my plan was starting to work, I turned into the Energizer Bunny of flexible thinking. At every opportunity, I verbalized flexible thoughts. While playing Monopoly, shooting baskets in the driveway, or eating a meal that wasn't my favorite, I started thinking out loud. Anyone who happened by probably thought I was a little goofy, but who cares? I was training my boys, and they were learning.

You can put this same technique to work in your household, teaching your child to be flexible by giving her a constant example of how *you* handle everyday challenges in a way that pleases God. When you're playing a game together, when you help with her homework, when a disappointing situation arises, open up a crack in your cranium and let her see how flexible thinking leads you to:

- Rely on God to help you handle daily challenges: "Guys, let's remember to pray for Grandma tonight. In fact, let's pray for her right now."
- Put things into proper perspective: "Well, I can always go to a movie some other time. It's no big deal."
- Let the little things go: "I'm not going to worry about that. I have so many things I can thank God for."
- Think of others ahead of yourself: "Curtis, go ahead and have the last cookie, buddy. I can have something else. No problem."
- Consider a different point of view: "Well, hang on, Britney. Let's try to look at it from Danielle's point of view."

Let your child hear you "love the Lord your God with all your heart and with all your soul and with all your *mind*" (Matthew 22:37, emphasis added).

In other words, think out loud.

Developing the Skill of Flexible Thinking

In addition to thinking out loud, you can actually teach your child to use flexible thoughts that will help him stay calm and make a good choice. For kids younger than eight, talking about thoughts is too abstract, so I like to call them flexible *words*. This works out fine because in order to say flexible words, they have to think them, so we're really also training their thoughts.

A Rubber Band or a Stick

Here's an easy way to get started. Sit your child down and show him a rubber band, stretching it in several directions. Then you might say, "Ryan, do you see how this rubber band can stretch and bend? That's because it's flexible. It doesn't break or get all mad when things change. Have you ever seen a rubber band throw a tantrum? Nope. A rubber band knows how to be flexible. Some people are flexible with their bodies and muscles — a gymnast, for instance — and while it's great to be flexible with your muscles, we want to be flexible with our thoughts. A thought is just something you say to yourself, like talking to yourself in your head. We want to have flexible thoughts, just like a rubber band."

Now pull out a dry stick or a pencil, anything long and hard that you don't mind breaking. Slowly start to bend it, and then ask your child what will happen if you bend it too far. Keep on bending it until it snaps. "That's right. It will break because the stick doesn't know how to be flexible. That's like getting all mad and throwing a tantrum when something doesn't go your way."

Explain that your child can choose to be flexible like a rubber band or get mad and break like the old stick. It all depends on whether he uses flexible thoughts or mad thoughts. Flexible thoughts will help him stay calm and be respectful and will lead to lots more fun. Mad thoughts lead to angry feelings and disrespectful actions and will get him in trouble.

The simple yet effective lesson gives your child a visual image of what it means to use flexible thinking. He sees that if he's flexible and doesn't get mad and "break" every time something doesn't go his way, he'll have a lot more fun.

Give your child a few examples of mad thoughts, such as *That's not fair!*, *You're so mean!*, and *You wreck everything!* Ask him if he thinks these are mad thoughts or flexible thoughts. Then give some examples of flexible thoughts, such as *It won't take that long*, *It's no big deal*, or *That's okay; I can do this later.* Ask him if he thinks these are mad thoughts or flexible thoughts. Over the next few days, look for opportunities to ask him about various examples of mad thoughts and flexible thoughts until he can easily tell the difference.

Flexible Thoughts in Practice

The same components you used to teach your child the skill of fast listening — *memorization* and *application* — are just as effective in teaching the skill of flexible thinking.

When I first teach a child the skill of flexible thinking, I select five flexible thoughts to get us started. (You can start with fewer for kids six or younger or for any child who has difficulty with memorization.) I usually begin with the first five flexible thoughts from the following list because they apply to many different situations.

FLEXIBLE THOUGHTS	
1. I should just do it.	13. How can I make the best of this situation?
2. It's no big deal.	14. Everyone makes mistakes.
3. It won't take long.	15. If I'm respectful, things will work out better.
4. The sooner I start, the sooner I'll be done.	16. He probably wasn't trying to make me mad.
5. That's okay. I can do it later.	17. If I argue, I'll just get in trouble.
6. Nobody gets his way all the time.	18. I want to treat them like I want to be treated.
7. I wonder how God wants me to handle this situation.	19. I can handle it.
8. Things don't always have to go my way.	20. Sometimes you just have to wait.
9. Even though I lost, I still had fun.	21. I can think of something else to do.
10. What's a solution that will work for everyone?	22. If I get stuck, I can ask for help.
11. I want to be smart and respectful.	23. God, please help me handle this the right way.
12. How can I think of the other person first?	24. You win some, you lose some.
	25. Everyone has to help out sometimes.

As you prepare to teach your own child, you'll want to identify the flexible thoughts that will be most helpful in the situations that are prompting his mad thoughts. You can choose from the list I've provided or make up a few of your own. You may want to read through the list with your child and allow him to identify the flexible thoughts he thinks will help him the most. When twelve-year-old Alex visited my office, he actually made up one of his own flexible thoughts: "It won't kill me." He was able to use that for almost any situation!

Once you've settled on a short list of flexible thoughts, write them down and help your child begin to memorize the list. By committing the thoughts to memory, your child will be able to quickly put them to work when a frustrating situation comes along. I've found that most kids can memorize three to five flexible thoughts in very little time. To help keep them fresh in his mind, you may want to quiz your child at bedtime to see how many flexible thoughts he can remember. Every time he says them all, give him a high five to let him know you're proud of his effort.

Once your child has memorized his flexible thoughts, help him practice applying them to different situations. Using common family scenarios and recent situations, just as you did with fast listening, practice flexible thinking together several times a week. In fact, you can practice how your child will combine flexible thinking with fast listening to respond respectfully to various situations.

Common scenarios you may want to practice include:

- Turning off an electronic activity, such as TV, video game, computer game
- Coming in from playing outside
- Losing at a sport or game
- Being asked to do a household chore
- Disagreeing with a sibling
- Making a mistake
- Coping with disappointment

- Having a request denied by Mom or Dad
- Going to a restaurant that's not a favorite
- Having a lot of homework

Remember to keep your practices short, fun, and encouraging so your child will remain interested and attentive.

Flexible Thinking in Action

Eight-year-old Michael used to throw monster fits whenever something didn't go his way, which was several times a day. When I first met him, Michael wouldn't have known a flexible thought if it came up and gave him a noogie. After a few weeks of practice, however, flexible thinking started to become a habit, and his flare-ups decreased significantly.

Here's an example of how I practiced flexible thoughts in one session with Michael:

Me:	Mike, do you remember your flexible thoughts?
Michael:	I think so.
Me:	Great. Let's hear them.
Michael:	I should fast listen. Um . . . it's no big deal. It won't take very long. The sooner I start, the quicker I'll get done, and . . . I forget.
Me:	Hey, that was four right off the bat. Good job. Let me help you with the last one. That's okay —
Michael:	(interrupting) I can do it later!
Me:	Perfect. Nice job learning them. Now, let's see if you can use your flexible thoughts in action. Let's pretend you're in the middle of something fun. What should we pick?
Michael:	Legos.
Me:	All right. Let's say you're in the middle of play-ing with your Legos and Mom asks you to stop

	because it's time for dinner. What flexible thought can you use?
Michael:	It's no big deal; I can do it later.
Me:	Hey, you combined two of them together. Very creative. Just for practice, can you think of another one?
Michael:	Um, I can always play with my Legos tomorrow.
Me:	Nice job. Now if you used those flexible thoughts, how would you feel?
Michael:	Pretty good.
Me:	And how would you use fast listening?
Michael:	I'd say, "Okay, Mom," and then come down for dinner.
Me:	Awesome. And how would that flexible thinking and fast listening work out for you?
Michael:	Well, I wouldn't get in trouble and I could probably play with Legos after dinner.
Me:	I think you're right, bud. What would happen if you used slow listening?
Michael:	I'd get in trouble.
Me:	Like what?
Michael:	Like I'd have to go to time-out or I couldn't play with Legos anymore.
Me:	That sounds about right. So what works better: slow listening or fast listening?
Michael:	Fast listening.

Can you see what a huge difference a few flexible thoughts can make?

If you review flexible thoughts with your child every day, she'll soon be able to rattle them right off, just as Michael did. This will make it easier for her to quickly apply them to many different situations. Repetition is the key. The more your child practices flexible thoughts, the sooner they'll become a part of her automatic thinking process, helping her control her temper and make respectful choices when things don't go her way.

It takes a little time to replace your child's old, negative thinking patterns with new, flexible thoughts, so don't get discouraged if it doesn't happen overnight. Remember, the problem is not the situation; the problem lies in the thoughts your child is thinking in that situation. As your child gradually replaces her mad thoughts with flexible thoughts, you'll notice a definite increase in respectful responses — and you'll both find your home a more pleasant place to be.

- Mad thoughts lead to angry responses, while flexible thoughts lead to respectful responses.

- Thinking out loud shows your child how you handle everyday challenges in a flexible way that pleases God.

- Memorizing three to five flexible thoughts will help your child quickly put them to work when a frustrating situation comes along.

- With practice, your child can combine flexible thinking with fast listening to respond respectfully to any situation.

- The more your child practices flexible thoughts, the sooner they'll become a part of her automatic thinking process.

1. Take a look at Proverbs 25:28, Ephesians 4:22-24, and Colossians 3:1-3. What do these passages tell us about the importance of learning to control our thoughts?

2. What mad thoughts currently seem to dominate your child's thinking in the midst of disappointing or frustrating situations?

3. What are some everyday scenarios in which you can think out loud to model flexible thinking for your child?

4. Describe an occasion when your child's inflexible, disrespectful behavior spoiled what could have been a pleasant family time. Identify a flexible thought your child could have used to handle the situation better.

5. Read Proverbs 29:11, Ephesians 4:26-27, and James 1:19-20. What do these verses tell us about how we, and our children, should respond to frustrating circumstances?

6. How do you generally respond to frustrating situations? What are your children learning from your example?

7. Do you know an adult who has never learned to be flexible? In what ways does this seem to have affected this person's marriage, career, family, and enjoyment of life?

8. Identify three to five flexible thoughts from the list on page 56 that you want to teach and practice with your child. What scenario will you use for your first practice session?

CHAPTER 5

How Can We Work This Out?

the skill of problem solving

When your child comes face-to-face with a problem, such as having a lot of homework or seeing his brother grab the TV remote before he can get to it, what's his initial reaction? If he's like many kids I meet, he probably tends to get frustrated and respond disrespectfully. Instead of trying to think of a good solution to the problem, many kids quickly resort to shouting, arguing, sulking, or annoying their sibling (not to mention driving their parents a few miles closer to crazy).

This is because few children are naturally gifted problem solvers. So it's up to us as their coaches to help our children develop their problem-solving skills. For kids younger than seven years old, the skills of fast listening and flexible thinking are sufficient for getting them started down the road of respect. But children who are seven and older — with the increased ability to understand the steps of the process — are ready to add problem-solving skills to their arsenal of respectful skills. Along with fast listening and flexible thinking, problem solving is an essential tool to help your child handle life's challenges in a creative and respectful way.

When I first met her, twelve-year-old Anna was not a top-notch problem solver, to say the least. Her mom described for me a typical scene in their home:

Anna:	Hey, Mom, can Olivia and Melissa come for a sleepover Friday night?
Mom:	Well, let me think. You have an early soccer game Saturday morning, and then Russell has a basketball tournament. How about if we do it another time?
Anna:	Awww, c'mon. We won't stay up too late. Let us do it.
Mom:	I think another weekend would be better.
Anna:	(starting to get mad) You never let me do anything! Russell had his friends over — why can't I?

Anna had just run headfirst into a problem without any problem-solving skills. Just like going skydiving without a parachute, a bumpy landing was inevitable.

Anna was unable to stop, think of various possible solutions, choose a good one, and pay attention to see if it worked. If she had been able to do these things, the scene might have looked more like this:

Anna:	Hey, Mom, can Olivia and Melissa come for a sleepover Friday night?
Mom:	Well, let me think. You have an early soccer game Saturday morning, and then Russell has a basketball tournament. How about if we do it another time?
Anna:	Like when?
Mom:	Well, let's take a look at the calendar and see if the next weekend would work.
Anna:	Okay. Hey, do you think maybe they could come over to play but not stay overnight?
Mom:	We might be able to do that.
Anna:	Great.

In both scenes, Anna faces the same problem: she will not be having a sleepover this Friday night. But the second scenario shows Anna talking respectfully to her mother, thinking of possible solutions, and being content with an answer that is different from what she had originally hoped for.

The second scene reveals how Anna could benefit from developing her skills at problem solving.

Turn Your Child into a Problem Solver

Like any new skill, problem solving requires some basic instruction and practice, but that's what a respect coach is for. If you think about it, your child learns complex skills all the time. Take baseball, for example. When stepping up to the plate to bat, the player needs to put his feet in the right spot, bend his knees, grip the bat properly, keep his rear elbow slightly raised, hold the bat at the correct angle, keep his eye on the ball, and swing at the right time. That's a lot to remember for a first-timer. However, with a little practice, most kids learn to do all of these things at the same time, without even thinking about it.

You can help your child do the same with problem solving.[4] With some clear instruction and a little practice, he can learn to problem solve automatically, without even thinking about it.

As with the other skills we've covered, helping your child memorize the right steps is key to preparing him to hit a home run every time he comes face-to-face with a problem. The acronym STAR—which stands for the steps Stop, Think, Act, and Review—will serve as your memory aid.[5] Let me explain how each step works, and then I'll demonstrate how I worked through each of the steps with Kevin, a ten-year-old who needed ideas for coping respectfully when his little sister bothered him.

Stop

When they encounter an obstacle that blocks the path to getting what they want, most kids barrel full speed ahead, trying to force their way to the goal. This is why their behavior so quickly goes off track. The solution involves learning to pause rather than stubbornly forging ahead. Your child needs to stop — resisting the urge to win at all costs — when she encounters a problem. Otherwise, the momentum of her anger, disappointment, or frustration will propel her to respond in a disrespectful and unproductive way.

Stopping can take any form that makes sense for your child's personality, such as setting a time to talk about the problem as a family, finding a quiet place to calm down, taking a few deep breaths, sitting down and closing her eyes, using a flexible thought, or simply reminding herself to stop and think.

When Kevin shared with me that he often got in trouble over how he responded when his little sister bugged him, we decided he needed a new way to deal with the situation:

Me:	The first step, Kevin, is to *stop*. This is really important, because if you don't stop when you're upset with Caitlyn, you end up doing something disrespectful, and that gets you in trouble. Has that ever happened?
Kevin:	(rolling his eyes) All the time.
Me:	Right. So what's a good way that you can stop and give yourself time to think?
Kevin:	I can just walk away?
Me:	That might work. Any other ideas?
Kevin:	Not really.
Me:	Let's think about this. Maybe you could take a couple deep breaths, go find a quiet place — away from Caitlyn — to calm down, or just remind yourself to stop and think. Do you like any of these ideas?
Kevin:	I like walking away or telling myself to stop and think.
Me:	Excellent. Let's remember those.

Think

The next step is really an exercise in creative thinking, with the goal of challenging your child to think up as many possible solutions to the problem as she can. The fact is, any given problem usually can be solved in a number of ways, but most kids need to practice thinking beyond the first idea that pops into their mind.

You might want to provide a paper and pen the first few times you work through this with your child. Ask her to list every possible solution she can think of, good or bad. Try to get at least three potential solutions. If your child runs out of ideas, offer a few of your own.

Here's how I explained this step to Kevin:

Me: The second step is to *think*. In other words, you want to come up with a good idea for how to handle the situation. What's a good idea for dealing with your sister when she bugs you?

Kevin: Tell her to stop.

Me: Well, possibly. It depends on how you do it. If you order her to stop, you might sound bossy. How do you usually tell her to stop?

Kevin: (raises his voice) "Stop it!"

Me: Hmmm. How respectful did that sound?

Kevin: Not very.

Me: Right. Let me give you a couple tips. First, it really helps if you say her name out loud. Second, you also say exactly what she's doing that bothers you. When you do these two things, Caitlyn knows that Mom and Dad will hear exactly what she's doing, and she's more likely to stop. For example, you could say "Caitlyn, would you please stop touching my papers when I'm doing my homework?" How does that idea sound to you?

Kevin: Pretty good.

Me:	You try it.
Kevin:	Caitlyn, will you please stop messing with my papers while I'm doing homework?
Me:	Perfect. You said that very respectfully, which is the key. Is there any way you could get in trouble for saying it like that?
Kevin:	Nope.
Me:	That's right. Now, what's another good idea?
Kevin:	Well, if it's something little, I guess I could just walk away.
Me:	If it's something little, ignoring her and walking away is an excellent idea. Any other ideas?
Kevin:	Go get Mom or Dad.
Me:	That's right. You've thought of several good ideas. Let's write those down. Great job.

Act

Once you've drafted a list of possible solutions, decide which solution, or combination of solutions, will make the best plan of action. Discuss the details of how the plan would work, and then encourage her to go ahead and try out the plan as an experiment.

Like most kids, Kevin really enjoyed plotting out a plan of action.

Me:	The third step in problem solving is to *act*. This means we need to put your ideas together into a plan and then try it out. Let's have a different plan for when your sister bugs you in a small, medium, or large way. Just like French fries.
Kevin:	Cool.
Me:	When she bugs you, your first step is to *stop*, by reminding yourself to stop and think. Right?
Kevin:	Right.

Me: Then, for small things, you can ignore her and walk away, using a flexible thought like, "It's no big deal." Sound good?

Kevin: Yeah, that will work.

Me: If she bugs you in a medium way, you can ask her to stop, using her name and saying exactly what she's doing that bugs you. How does that sound?

Kevin: Okay.

Me: If she keeps bugging you, I'd suggest that you ask her to stop one more time, with a little stronger tone but still not shouting or sounding disrespectful. Let's hear you try.

Kevin: Caitlyn, I asked you to stop touching my papers while I'm doing my homework. *Please* stop it.

Me: Good job. That sounded firm but not disrespectful. Way to go. Now, if she still keeps bugging you, what should you do?

Kevin: Get Mom or Dad.

Me: Great idea. I suggest that you *walk away* and get Mom or Dad instead of just shouting for them. Then you have no chance of getting in trouble. Sound like a good plan?

Kevin: Yeah.

Me: For large things, like if she hits you or kicks you, then you firmly tell her to stop and then go get Mom or Dad.

Kevin: Okay.

Me: Now let's practice once more. I'll pretend to be your sister and bug you in small, medium, and large ways. You show me how you would use your plan.

Review

Both in your practice sessions and after your child initially tries out her plan in real life, make a point to evaluate the outcome. Encourage her to learn from the experiment. If it works, super. If it doesn't work, find out why and adjust the solution to fix the problem.

After our final round of practice, Kevin and I discussed the effectiveness of his plan:

Me:	The last step in our problem-solving process is to *review*. So how did your plan work in practice?
Kevin:	Pretty good.
Me:	How do you think it would work with Caitlyn?
Kevin:	It would work fine.
Me:	Can you think of any way that you could get in trouble if you were to use this plan just the way we practiced it?
Kevin:	Nope.
Me:	Me neither. You did every step very respectfully. So here's our plan. You go home and use this plan if Caitlyn bugs you. Next time I see you, you can tell me how it worked. If we need to, we can make some adjustments. Sound good?
Kevin:	Yep.
Me:	Great. And remember to keep your words and attitude respectful — that's the key. The more friendly and respectful you are to Caitlyn, the more friendly and respectful she'll be to you.
Kevin:	Yeah, I know.
Me:	All right, buddy. I know you'll do a great job.

In less than twenty minutes, Kevin had stopped complaining about his sister and instead was investing his energy in solving his problem. He had decided to ignore minor irritations, ask his sister politely to stop when the irritations were moderate, and get help from parents when she didn't stop or when the irritations were major. Not bad for a ten-year-old kid.

It's amazing to hear the ideas kids come up with when you empower them to solve a problem instead of trying to fix it for them. When you teach your child the STAR method of problem solving and practice it regularly with her, I think you'll be impressed by how quickly she becomes adept at finding good solutions for the problems she encounters each day.

Problem Solving On the Go

I find STAR to be the most effective approach to problem solving when there is time to sit down and talk through the situation. However, sometimes you don't have the luxury of working through all the steps; sometimes you need immediate resolution. This is a perfect time for what I call problem solving on the go. Essentially it's an abbreviated approach to finding an answer everyone can live with, and it involves only two steps.[6]

Step One: Make an Empathetic Comment

In order to engage your child in finding a solution, you must first get past his angry defenses. (This is especially important when he thinks *you* are the problem, which is quite often the case.) In order to accomplish this, you're going to do something sneaky: You're going to agree with your child. Demonstrating empathy is absolutely vital for problem solving on the go. In fact, the second step is almost certain to fail if you skimp here.

Empathy involves looking at a situation from the other person's perspective. So when your child runs up against a problem, mentally trade places for a moment. Remember what it was like to be a pre-hormonal twelve-year-old girl coping with peer pressure or a disappointed seven-year-old boy whose after-school playtime plans have just been dashed against the rocks of an afternoon of homework.

Then, along with a reassuring squeeze, give voice to your child's feeling of frustration or disappointment by making an empathetic comment. You can do it in one sentence, expressed in a tone that shows that you understand how he feels and why. For example, you might say:

- "Hey, pal, I know homework isn't much fun. I can see that you really don't feel like doing it right now."
- "Oh sweetie, it's really hard to stop playing when you're having such a good time."
- "Picking up the dog poop isn't your favorite job, huh? Well, it's not mine either, so I understand how you feel."
- "I know it's frustrating to stop right in the middle of a game. I find that hard sometimes too."

I have a friend who's outstanding at making empathetic comments. It's amazing to watch how her kids respond when she immediately identifies with how they feel when faced with a problem. How can they argue when she shows that she understands exactly how they feel? All they can say is, "Yeah, that's right."

An empathetic comment shows your child that you are for him and not against him. You do understand his feelings. You're on his side. This assurance immediately helps calm the situation and stop the escalation of resentment.

Step Two: Engage in Mutual Problem Solving

Once you've shown your child that you understand where he's coming from, the next step is to encourage him to use the problem-solving skills he's been practicing. You can do this with just one simple question: "What's a good idea for how we can handle this?" Because you took the time to show that you understand his feelings, he'll be more willing to think of solutions. Plus, by using the word *we*, you communicate your willingness to help.

This is mutual problem solving, which means you will do it together.

This approach is especially helpful with children who become rigid and easily frustrated. Instead of forcing a head-on collision by confronting him with a rule, you join with him in finding a good solution to the problem. Your child may need a bit of extra help in moving toward a solution, especially if emotions are running high. If your child suggests an unrealistic solution, there's no need to argue with him. Just calmly point out the impracticality of that solution and encourage him to think of another one. If he runs out of ideas, then you can suggest a solution that might work.

The emotional tone you set heavily influences your child's level of emotional control. By remaining calm and focused on finding a positive solution rather than wasting energy on arguing, you help your child to do the same. If your child won't make an effort to think of positive ways to resolve the problem, then you'll need to suggest the solution that will be used. If he refuses to go with your decision, a negative consequence may be in order. (We'll discuss negative consequences in part 3.)

The idea here is to equip your child to become skilled at solving problems even in a stressful situation. You can always review the situation later with your child, using the STAR steps to consider the effectiveness of your solution and to decide on a plan for handling any similar problems that may arise.

It's Fun to Be a Problem Solver

Whether it involves all four steps in the STAR approach or getting creative with problem solving on the go, the more experience your child gains, the more comfortable she'll become at solving problems on her own. All it takes is instruction, practice, and encouragement. When you see your child make an effort to find a solution, let her know you're proud of her choice to focus on the solution instead of the problem.

And remember that problem solving doesn't have to be particularly serious or complex. Our boys have solved countless problems with simple solutions, such as "rock, paper, scissors" or "pick a number from

1 to 10." Encourage your child to find answers that not only work but also bring out her creative or fun-loving side. Boost her confidence in her own problem-solving skills by inviting her to think of solutions for some of the ordinary family problems that pop up from time to time, such as running out of everyone's favorite cereal or deciding on what games to play for family night.

Together with fast listening and flexible thinking, your child can use the STAR steps and problem solving on the go to respond creatively and respectfully to any type of home, school, or peer situation.

Every problem has a good solution. Your job is to help your child learn to find it.

- Problem solving is an essential tool to help your child handle life's challenges in a creative and respectful way.
- With some clear instruction and a little practice, your child can learn to problem solve automatically.
- The STAR approach to problem solving involves four steps: Stop, Think, Act, and Review.
- Problem solving on the go involves making an empathetic comment and asking your child, "What's a good idea for how we can handle this?"
- When you stay calm and focused during the problem-solving process, you help your child to do the same.

1. Read Proverbs 14:8, 15:22, 19:2, and 21:5. How does taking the time to follow specific problem-solving steps help your child honor God in the way he responds to everyday problems?

2. How skilled is your child at finding good solutions to problems? What problem-solving mistakes does he usually make?

3. Describe a recent situation in which your child could have used problem-solving skills. How might the outcome have been different if he already knew the basics of problem solving?

4. Which of the four STAR steps will be the most difficult for your child?

5. How do you think your child will respond to problem solving on the go? What steps can you take to avoid arguing with your child and remain calm?

6. If you practice them regularly, what impact will these problem-solving skills have on your family relationships?

7. On a scale of 1 to 10, with 10 being "great," how would your child rate your ability to see things from his point of view? What difference will it make if you start using empathetic comments more regularly?

8. Identify at least one family problem that you can tackle with the STAR problem-solving steps right away. Describe a situation in which you anticipate needing to use problem solving on the go.

2

Turn On Respectful Behavior

I can live for two months on a good compliment.

MARK TWAIN

Pleasant words are a honeycomb, sweet to the soul and healing to the bones.

PROVERBS 16:24

CHAPTER 6

Looking for Gold

the art of making respect fun

D o you have fond memories of a favorite teacher from your school
days? My sixth-grade teacher, Mr. Exner, reigned as my hero
among teachers. He was the first teacher I had who motivated us to
complete our work by offering the incentive of classroom dollars. He
had his mug shot plastered right in the middle of them. These Exner
Rubles, as he used to call them in honor of his Russian heritage, could
be used to purchase small snacks and fun classroom supplies.

This year my oldest son has an entertaining teacher, one who eats
and breathes social studies. His blankets at home were probably sewn by
Betsy Ross. He does funny, over-the-top things in class, such as breaking out in song and dressing up like a pilgrim, to keep the students
engaged in the learning process. He's currently Jacob's favorite teacher
because he makes learning fun.

With all due respect to the social studies teachers of the world, I
figure that if you can make social studies fun, then you can make just
about anything fun. And as your child's respect coach, that's your objective. You want to help your child develop an enthusiasm for respectful
behavior. You want him to see that respectful behavior is fun and that it
will always work out better than disrespectful behavior. You want him
to notice that it makes your home a fun place to be and your family

more fun to be with because it increases the enjoyable experiences you all have together.

The Rewards of Respect

Right now, your child may have a somewhat twisted perspective of respectful behavior, viewing it solely as a royal pain in the gluteus maximus. In other words, she may see respectful behavior as all work and no fun. This is actually backward. Many of our kids could use a little "renewing of their minds" (see Romans 12:2) on this topic to view the issue of respect more accurately.

First, we need to help our kids see that being respectful to others is a natural extension of our relationship to God and our obedience to his command that we love our neighbor as we love ourselves. Jesus said, "Do to others as you would have them do to you" (Luke 6:31). He knew that treating others respectfully, or as you would like to be treated, not only gives you the inner satisfaction of knowing you are obeying God but also helps you achieve close family relationships and strong friendships.

Second, while it takes practice to develop the habit of respectful behavior and it sometimes requires compromise or sacrifice, respectful choices usually are not all that difficult.

Third, being respectful doesn't mean all work and no fun. Sometimes it just means work *before* fun, which is something we all must learn.

Fourth, we want our kids to learn that making respectful choices is the only way to turn on the positives, whether that means close relationships or increased privileges. In fact, without respectful behavior, all fun privileges will surely disappear. As soon as your child begins to realize this, her behavior will begin to change.

Put the Rewards in the Right Place

This concept was nicely illustrated by five-year-old Aidan, who used to have a hard time staying in bed at night. He would creep out of bed and sneak around the corner as if he were a secret agent, spying on his parents through the upstairs banisters. Other times, his bladder would mysteriously shrink to the size of a thimble and he'd desperately need to visit the bathroom every ten minutes. Another frequent problem was his recurring dry throat, which became terribly parched if sips of water weren't supplied at regular five-minute intervals. In short, Aidan didn't want to stay in bed. What he wanted was his parents' attention. Brian and Maria, Aidan's parents, had tried yelling, reprimanding, and even confiscating favorite toys in their attempts to convince Aidan to stay in bed.

We decided to try a different approach.

Because Aidan's bedtime antics were geared to get his parents' attention, we decided to use that attention to persuade him to stay in bed. Brian and Maria set a timer in his room and told him that if he stayed in bed until the timer went off, one of them would immediately come to his room and spend a couple minutes with him. If Aidan got out of bed before the timer went off, his parents would march him straight back to his room — without conversation or giving any positive attention — reset the timer, and remind him that they would come to see him only if he stayed in bed until the timer rang.

Brian and Maria started by setting the timer for thirty seconds and leaving the room. Aidan stayed in bed, eagerly waiting for the timer to ring. When it did, Maria immediately came in, praised him for doing a great job, and gave him a little back rub. She then set the timer for sixty seconds and reminded Aidan to stay in bed. They continued this process, gradually increasing the time on the timer after each short visit. After about forty-five minutes, Aidan was fast asleep. Aidan's parents continued to use the timer each night, and by the end of the week, Aidan rarely needed to be reminded to stay in bed. Each night his parents set the timer for longer periods of time, and they soon discontinued using it altogether.

The approach we used with Aidan may seem counterintuitive if you are used to relying solely on negative consequences to change your child's behavior. That's what Brian and Maria had been doing, and it clearly wasn't working. They could have continued punishing Aidan, but instead we took all the attention away from getting out of bed and connected it with staying in bed. When we put the attention in the right place, we got a much better result.

I've met a few parents who wrestle with the concept of rewarding a child just for behaving as instructed. Their philosophy is that kids should do the right thing simply because it's the right thing to do. This thinking reveals a misunderstanding of the role rewards play in the way children learn to make the choices that ultimately shape their habits.

For example, I don't know too many eight-year-olds who do their homework so they can go to college. They do it because they won't be able to play until it gets done. While your child enjoys receiving a good grade on her report card, she needs immediate motivation to help her make the daily positive choices that will ultimately bring the long-term rewards. As she continually experiences both the immediate and long-term rewards that positive choices bring, these choices gradually turn into positive habits.

We can also consider the example given to us by the ultimate parent: God. The Scripture says, "He will take great delight in you, he will quiet you with his love, he will rejoice over you with singing" (Zephaniah 3:17). We glimpse the Father's great delight in his Son when we read of Jesus' baptism. Matthew 3:16-17 tells us that God parted the heavens and the Spirit of God descended on Jesus like a dove and lighting on him. Then he heard his Father say, "This is my Son, whom I love; with him I am well pleased." How's that for some heavenly encouragement!

The Bible makes it clear that God delights in rewarding his children when they obey him (see Jeremiah 17:10; Matthew 16:27; Ephesians 6:8). He's rooting for you in the same way a proud father beams with joy when his daughter takes her first steps or learns to ride a bike. He rejoices in heaven when we choose to obey him.

As we follow the example of our heavenly Father, we can let our kids know we're proud of them when they choose the right path. We can rejoice when they make good decisions, just as our heavenly Father rejoices over us. Our children need a healthy balance of firm correction and joyful encouragement. That's how God parents us, and that's how he wants us to parent our children.

Mining for Gold

As we're thinking about how to motivate our children to consistently choose respectful behavior, we want to be aware of the impact our own words and attitudes have on the choices they make and the way they think about themselves.

In *Developing the Leaders Around You*, well-known leadership author John Maxwell tells the story of the time a reporter asked motivational expert Dale Carnegie how he had managed to hire more than forty-three millionaires throughout his career. That's quite a few. Keep in mind, however, that these people were not millionaires when Carnegie hired them. As the result of working with Carnegie, these people developed into effective leaders and ultimately became financially successful. Carnegie pondered the question for a moment and then answered, "[People] are developed the same way gold is mined. Several tons of dirt must be moved to get an ounce of gold. But you don't go into the mine looking for dirt. You go in looking for the gold."[7]

With that insight in mind, I have a question: When God blessed you with a child, what did he give you? Did he give you a lump of dirt? In your heart, you know the answer is no. He gave you a gold nugget. That's right, a gold nugget that he made himself. Here's what David wrote when he realized that he too was one of God's precious gold nuggets:

> For you created my inmost being;
>> you knit me together in my mother's womb.
> I praise you because I am fearfully and wonderfully made;
>> your works are wonderful,
>> I know that full well.

My frame was not hidden from you
> when I was made in the secret place.
When I was woven together in the depths of the earth,
> your eyes saw my unformed body.
All the days ordained for me
> were written in your book
> before one of them came to be. (Psalm 139:13-16)

Now, occasionally your gold nugget may get so covered with dirt that you can't quite see the glow of the treasure underneath. But your job is to brush off the dirt and bring forth the beautiful, unique gold nugget that lies within. And to do that, you have to look for the gold.

Look for the Gold, Not the Dirt

Without realizing it, most of us parents are more aware of the dirt in our children's lives than the gold. Make no mistake, there's plenty of dirt to be found. Talking back, arguing, sibling fighting — all this is dirt. But you don't find the gold by looking for the dirt. All you find is more dirt.

Why are most of us so focused on the dirt? Maybe it's because our parents watched for the dirt in us, or perhaps it's because looking at other people's dirt takes our mind off our own. No matter what the reason, you can break that bad habit and teach yourself to look for the gold in your children. You want your children to realize they are God's precious gold nuggets, who occasionally have a bad day and make a wrong choice, just like the rest of us.

In the midst of day-to-day parenting and with all the things we want to teach our children in just a few short years, it's tempting to focus primarily on the dirt, on those things we want our kids to *stop* doing. Most of us have been doing this our whole parenting lives. But as we consider how to bring out the best in our kids, I'd encourage you to try a new strategy: Focus instead on what you want your child to *start* doing. Try this brief exercise:

INSTEAD OF . . .	I'D LIKE MY CHILD TO . . .
arguing	_____
hitting a sibling	_____
shouting	_____
quitting when he loses a game	_____
name calling when he's mad	_____

Here's how I would complete each statement:

INSTEAD OF . . .	I'D LIKE MY CHILD TO . . .
arguing	say, "Okay, Mom," and do it (fast listening)
hitting a sibling	respectfully state what he wants, or come and get me
shouting	talk with respectful words and volume level
quitting when he loses a game	use a flexible thought and keep on trying
name calling when he's mad	say how he feels in a respectful way

When you focus solely on decreasing your child's disrespectful behavior, he learns only half a lesson. His primary motivation is to behave in order to avoid punishment. However, as soon as the threat of punishment is gone, the disrespectful behavior immediately returns. Why? Because he still thinks that the disrespectful behavior is worth doing. You've tried to move him away from a bad habit without motivating him toward a good habit.

An effective coach will teach the other half of the lesson as well. You want your child to learn that being respectful *always* works out the best. When your child is respectful to others, he experiences the joy and satisfaction of obeying God, contributing to a happy family, making friends, turning on the privileges, and feeling great. What could be better than that? When he realizes how awesome respectful behavior is, you won't have to punish him into it; he'll want to do it on his own.

Not too long ago, I was asked to participate in a Sunday morning parenting series at Christian Life Center in Dayton, Ohio. Lora and the boys came along and heard me talk about looking for the gold instead of the dirt. The next day, it so happened that Lora and I found ourselves getting frustrated with Jacob about some minor thing he'd done. His brother, Luke, was in the bathroom at the time, eavesdropping on our conversation with Jacob. Suddenly his voice emerged through the bathroom door, sounding like a parent shouting through cupped hands from the bleachers at a sporting event: "Jacob, be gold, not dirt!"

We all stopped, looked at each other, and burst out laughing. Ever since that day, "Be gold, not dirt" has served as a humorous catchphrase that instantaneously provokes laughter for the family and helps us put things in perspective. For my boys, this phrase represents the fact that they are responsible for choosing their behavior and that gold nugget behavior is always the way to go.

Just today, Jacob came home from summer football practice, limping and dog-tired but beaming with pride. He told me how during their grueling conditioning drills the coach had used him as an example of the kind of hard work it would take to make the starting lineup. I could just hear the coach shouting at the top of his lungs, "That's the kind of effort I'm looking for. That's what I want on my starting lineup. Good job, Cartmell." Simple words. Big effect. Exhausted as he was, Jacob couldn't wait to go back for more.

Jacob's coach was looking for the gold.

Make Your Gold Nugget Shine

Thirteen-year-old Tyler's argumentative behavior at home prompted his parents to make an appointment with me. In our meetings together, what stood out to me was Tyler's relationship with his mother, Jennifer. The two of them clashed more than paisley and stripes, and Jennifer had a way of making Tyler so mad that he looked as if he'd burst into a million pieces.

Jennifer: Tyler, why don't you tell him what you did?

Tyler:	(scowling) I don't want to.
Jennifer:	(sarcastically) Oh no, I want you to go ahead and tell him. Tell him how you talked to me last night. I'm sure he'd like to hear about it. I'm sure he'd like to hear the names you called me. Go ahead.
Me:	Tyler, would you like to talk about it?
Tyler:	(while looking at his shoes) No.
Jennifer:	You know why he doesn't want to talk about it? Because he doesn't want to tell you how rudely he treated his mother, that's why.
Tyler:	(close to shouting) Yeah, well I stopped, didn't I? I told you I wanted to calm down, didn't I? But you wouldn't stop yelling at me. You wouldn't let it go.
Jennifer:	I wouldn't need to yell if you didn't talk so disrespectfully to me and everyone in the family. Do you see how he talks to me?

As you may have gathered, Jennifer was quite proficient at pointing out the dirt, but she was not in the habit of looking for the gold. As a result, she had severely damaged her relationship with her son. Conversely, nine-year-old Madison also had a problem with argumentative behavior, but because her parents, Doug and Kathy, had learned to look for the gold, their visits to my office had an unmistakably different tone.

Doug:	Well, we had a few rough days this past couple of weeks that we should talk about, but there were several good days, too.
Kathy:	Yes, that's right. I even wrote a few things down so I wouldn't forget them. Maddie did a wonderful job of fast listening a few mornings before school, and she's been great about getting her homework done.

Me:	Maddie, is that right?
Madison:	I guess so.
Me:	How do you feel about that?
Madison:	(smiling) I feel pretty good.
Me:	Well, congratulations for handling those situations well. Why don't you tell me about some of the times that didn't go so well?
Madison:	I forget.
Kathy:	Do you want me to tell him?
Madison:	Okay.
Kathy:	Do you remember the time when you threw a big fit because you didn't want to clean your room?
Madison:	Oh, now I do.
Doug:	You did calm down eventually, so we have to give you credit for that. In the past, you would have thrown a fit for much longer.
Kathy:	Yes, that's true. But I'd like to help Maddie learn to handle things without getting so angry.
Me:	Maddie, would you like to work on that?
Madison:	Yeah, that's a good idea.

Do you see the difference? Jennifer was focused on the dirt, which meant Tyler focused on it too. Doug and Kathy were looking for the gold, which made Madison see it too — and want to find more of it.

If your child thinks he's a lump of dirt, then he'll act like one. But when you help him realize he really is a gold nugget — God's treasured gold nugget — then he will begin to shine. And you will rejoice with him, just as his Father in heaven will be rejoicing.

God gave you his own precious gold nuggets to love and guide for a few short years. If you have older children, you already know how quickly those years speed by. At the time of this writing, my boys are eleven and thirteen years old, and I am painfully aware of how fast the time goes. Lora and I cherish every minute of being with our two boys and would press the rewind button back to when they were four and six years old in a heartbeat. But children don't come with a rewind button. With the time you have left, your job is to gently brush away the dirt and bring out the special brand of gold that God has placed in the nuggets he gave you. But in order to do that, you have to learn to look for the gold.

The next few chapters reveal key principles for helping your child make the connection between respectful behavior and the benefits it brings. As your child learns that treating others the way God tells us to is always the best choice, you'll begin to notice there's a little less dirt in your house and a whole lot more gold.

- You want your child to learn that respectful behavior will always work out better than disrespectful behavior.
- When mining for gold, you don't go in looking for the dirt. You look for the gold.
- A new strategy for increasing respectful behavior is to focus on what you want your child to start doing.
- When your child realizes how awesome respectful behavior is, he'll want to do it on his own.
- If your child thinks he's a lump of dirt, he'll act like one; but when you help him realize that he really is a gold nugget, he'll begin to shine.

1. Read Jeremiah 17:10, Ephesians 6:8, and Matthew 6:3-4,6,17-18. What do these verses tell us about how God responds when we make choices that please him? How can we apply this idea to our kids when they make respectful choices?

2. Do you think your child is convinced that respectful behavior works out better than disrespectful behavior? Explain.

3. How are you teaching your child that respectful behavior always works out far better than disrespectful behavior?

4. What difference might it make in your family when you focus on the respectful behavior you want your child to start instead of just focusing on the disrespectful behavior you want her to stop?

5. Whether at the office or in your family/peer relationships, which motivates you more: the threat of getting in trouble, or the joy of a compliment or reward?

6. Did your parents look for the gold or the dirt when you were a child? What impact did that have on your view of yourself? On your behavior? On your relationship with them?

7. Would your child say that you more often look for the gold or the dirt? Why might he give that answer?

8. Think of a specific behavior you'd like to see change in your child. How might your approach differ if you're looking for gold rather than dirt?

CHAPTER 7

The Lesson of the Circles

the respect-privilege connection

Nine-year-old Ian suffered from a problem I've seen in my office a hundred times: When playing video games, he cosmically became "one" with the game. While this probably enhanced his game-time performance, it had a negative impact on the rest of his life. Whenever his parents asked him to turn off the game, Ian couldn't seem to wrench himself away from the game controller. Compelled to eke out a few more precious minutes of playing time, he often resorted to disrespectful measures, such as ignoring, whining, and arguing.

Ian's disrespectful behavior was motivated by his desire to gain a privilege. He was about to have a face-to-face encounter with the respect-privilege connection.

Making the Respect-Privilege Connection

Most kids I meet seem to have only a vague knowledge of the United States Constitution and the Bill of Rights. When I ask them about it, they respond, "Bill who?" Therefore, they've concluded that any privileges they enjoy—such as watching TV, riding bicycles, or playing with dolls—are part of the civil liberties granted to all children. Weren't the founding fathers committed to guaranteeing our unalienable rights, such as life, liberty, and the pursuit of PlayStation?

You should see the wide-eyed looks of disbelief when I break the bad news that none of the framers of the Constitution had an Xbox. One of my best friends, Dr. Steve Vincent, told me he also regularly finds it necessary to explain to kids the difference between rights and privileges. Steve spells out their rights in simple language: food, shelter, clothing, a basic education, and safety. Everything else is a bonus.

Why is it so critical to help our children see this distinction between rights and privileges? Because we want them to realize that privileges are gained not through claiming our rights under the Constitution but through respectful behavior. We want our children to learn that treating people respectfully (as God wants us to) will always work out better than treating them disrespectfully. To put it in language that kids will clearly understand, the child who treats others respectfully will experience the benefits that only respectful behavior can bring. Those benefits include knowing in your heart that you're obeying God, being a Christlike example in the world, developing close family and peer relationships, and experiencing various other fun privileges.

The Lesson of the Circles

In my discussion with Ian, I used a simple yet effective method to help him more fully grasp the implications of the respect-privilege connection. I call it "the lesson of the circles," and you can use it just as effectively with your child. All you need is the ability to make a circle with the thumb and first finger of each hand (like an "okay" sign).

Me:	Ian, I have a really important lesson for us to talk about today. It's called the lesson of the circles. Are you ready?
Ian:	Okay.
Me:	(curving the fingers of my left hand to make a circle) Here's the first circle, your respect circle. You can take it high (lifting the circle high above

my head), which means you are fast listening, using flexible thoughts, and treating others in a friendly way. Or you could take your respectful circle low (lowering the circle to my knees), which means you are arguing, slow listening, throwing tantrums, and treating others disrespectfully. Do you get the idea?

Ian: Uh huh.

Me: Now, who controls your respect circle?

Ian: I do?

Me: That's right. You are the only one who makes it go up or down. I would love for your circle to be up, but you are the only one who controls your circle. Now (curving the fingers of my right hand to make a circle), do you know what this second circle is?

Ian: No.

Me: This is your fun circle. This circle stands for all of your fun and privileges. Remember, I said *all* of your fun and privileges. Everything fun you do is in this circle. Name three things you do for fun.

Ian: Video games, my cars, and playing outside.

Me: All those things are in this circle. Every fun thing. Now, who do you think controls your fun circle?

Ian: I do.

Me: I hate to break it to you, pal, but you really don't. Your mom and dad control your fun circle. All the fun things you have and do are things that Mom and Dad either bought for you or allow you to do. For example, they can let you watch TV (moving right-hand circle up), or they can take that privilege away (moving right-hand circle down). Is that true?

Ian: Yeah, I guess that's right.

Me: So where would you like your fun circle to be: up or down?

Ian: Up.

Me: I agree. I would love your fun circle to be up, all the way up to the ceiling! So we have our two circles, our respect circle and our fun circle, right?

Ian: Yep.

At this point, Ian understood what each of the circles represented. Now it was time to teach him the relationship between the circles.

Me: Now, here's the lesson of the circles. Your mom and dad love you so much that they want you to learn how important it is to treat other people respectfully (lifting the respect circle high). That's one important way you obey God — by treating other people the way you'd like them to treat you. Respectfully, right?

Ian: Right.

Me: It's also a great way to make friends and have an awesome family. Would you like that?

Ian: Yeah, that sounds good.

Me: So to help you learn that important lesson, Mom and Dad are going to take the fun circle and hook it on to your respect circle (linking the two circles together). That way, if your respect circle goes up, what happens to your fun circle? (raising both circles)

Ian: It goes up.

Me: Right, which is great. But if your respect circle goes down, what happens to your fun circle? (lowering both circles)

Ian: It goes down.

Me: Yes, and that's sad. Is there any way that your fun circle can go up if your respect circle is down?

Ian: No.

Me: That's right. What is the only way in the universe to make your fun circle go up?

Ian: If my respect circle goes up?

Me: That's right, buddy. So the lesson of the circles is that your respect circle and your fun circle are always hooked together. And the only way to make your fun circle go up is to make your respect circle go up first.

Making the Circles Go Up

Within less than five minutes, Ian and his mother, Angela, had learned the lesson of the circles. Then we discussed how the respect-privilege connection applied to his video game situation. I told Ian there are three things he has to do if he wants to play a video game (and the same is true for any privilege your child wants to participate in):

1. Start right
2. Stay on right
3. Stop right

"It's just like riding a bike," I told Ian. "You have to be able to get on your bike without falling off, stay on your bike without falling off, and stop it without crashing. If you fall off or crash every time you ride, then you'll have to stop riding or put the training wheels back on.

"In the same way, you have to start your video game the right way, by asking permission to play or playing only when your mom has said it's okay. You have to stay on right, by treating people and property respectfully while playing the game. And you have to stop right, by using fast listening when you're asked to turn the game off."

Ian's biggest challenge was in following the third rule. He wasn't stopping right, which, according to the respect-privilege connection, meant he would lose his video game privilege. I wanted to help him fix that.

Thinking back to previous chapters, what respect skills do you think Ian needed to put to work? He needed to use flexible thinking and fast listening. So I laid out a three-step plan for him to follow when his mom asked him to turn off a video game:

1. Think, *That's okay. I can play later. Right now I need to fast listen.*
2. Say, "Okay, Mom," or ask a question in a respectful way.
3. Do what Mom said to do.

It took about ten minutes to teach Ian this plan for using flexible thinking and fast listening. He and his mom spent the rest of the session practicing it together, which Ian found rather fun. He soon showed us that he could do his plan in rehearsal without a flaw. We agreed that Ian and his mother would practice this plan at home every day for one week.

Then we made a clear connection between Ian's respect circle and fun circle: If Ian chose to use this plan at home, he could continue to have the privilege of playing his video games. Super. However, if he argued when asked to turn off his video game, then his game privilege would immediately be suspended for a day or two. In order to regain his privilege, he would have to practice his plan several times in order to show his mom that he could do it. (We'll talk more about positive practice in chapter 13.) If he was successful in rehearsals, then he would earn another chance to play his video games in real life. And if Ian chose to throw a fit about losing his game privilege, he'd receive a negative consequence, such as being sent to time-out (see Strategy Three), and his opportunity to earn back his privilege would be delayed another day.

As you can see, this plan involved no arguments and no yelling on Angela's part. We simply showed Ian how fast listening and flexible thinking would make his fun circle go up and how disrespectful behavior would make it go down.

Ian learned quickly that the "start right, stay on right, stop right" rule was no joke. He lost his video game privilege within the first two days and had to earn it back through positive rehearsals. Within two weeks, Angela proudly commented on the drastic improvement she had noticed in Ian's video game behavior.

Highlighting the Benefits of Respect

Because kids tend to just plow through their days at full speed, it's often helpful if we as parents help them pause to evaluate the effectiveness of their choices. Prompting them to "check their circles" — are they high or low? — is an easy way to help them get in the habit of assessing their own behavior and noting the respect-privilege connection.

I often ask kids in my office to rate their circles on a scale of 1 to 10 (10 being the highest). If their circles are high (a rating of 7 or higher), I congratulate them, and we talk about how they can keep them high. If they're low, we come up with ideas to make them higher.

Remind Them Where the Fun Comes From

Occasionally when your child is about to engage in a fun activity, such as watching a video or playing with his friends, you may want to give him a little squeeze and remind him that this fun activity is not happening by accident. Angela found this an effective strategy for reminding Ian about the benefits of respectful behavior:

Ian:	Mom, can I play a video game?
Angela:	Sure, honey. Hey, Ian, can I ask you a question?
Ian:	Yeah.
Angela:	Where is your fun circle right now?
Ian:	Pretty high.
Angela:	What number would you say?

Ian:	A nine.
Angela:	A nine! That's *very* high. Why do you think it's so high?
Ian:	I don't know.
Angela:	Well, there's only one way your fun circle can go up, and that's if your respect circle takes it up. I think you've been super-respectful today. You've been doing great with fast listening, and you worked really hard on your homework.
Ian:	Thanks.
Angela:	The reason you can play a video game right now is because you've been very respectful today, so keep up the good work, okay?
Ian:	Okay, Mom.

Ian was having fun because his circles were high. Why were his circles high? Because he was choosing to be respectful.

What a difference it makes when kids can see for themselves the connection between fun and respect!

Make Time for Reflection

Because we want our boys to become convinced for themselves that trusting God and following his commands is the absolute best path for their lives, Lora and I have made it a goal to spend a few minutes every week reflecting with them on their recent choices. Sometimes we do this together during a family time; other times we spend time with each boy individually, casually chatting together on the couch, seizing the right moment during a car ride, taking them out to breakfast, or talking quietly as we tuck them into bed.

Lora and I value the chance to explore their reflections about the choices they have made during the past week and to help them see how those choices are a part of their Christian growth. Our hope is that these discussions will help our boys be aware of the lessons God is constantly teaching them. While our discussions can range over many areas — such as family relationships, priorities, friendships, and peer pressures — we also talk about the issue of respect.

Me: Well, how do you think things have been going lately, pal?

Jacob: Fine.

Me: How do you think you've been doing at being respectful?

Jacob: Pretty good, really.

Me: Yeah, I think so too. I think you've been really respectful with Luke, and you've been listening great to Mom and me too.

Jacob: Yeah, thanks.

Me: What do you think God thinks about that?

Jacob: I think he likes it.

Me: Yeah, I'm sure he does. How does God want us to treat each other in our family?

Jacob: Respectfully.

Me: Sure. What are some ways you've been doing that?

Jacob: Well, I've been listening, talking respectfully, staying caught up on my homework, trying to be a good example at school.

Me: Buddy, that's awesome. I'm proud of you for obeying God in all those areas of your life. Hey, what happens to our family when we treat each other the way God wants us to?

Jacob: We all get along. We have fun together.

Me: Yeah, we sure do. It's a lot better than fighting and arguing, that's for sure. You know how Proverbs tells us to stay on God's path? (see Proverbs 4:26-27)

Jacob: Yeah.

Me: What do you think about God's path?

Jacob:	It makes a lot of sense to stay on it.
Me:	I think so too.

These discussions are sometimes shorter, sometimes longer, but always meaningful. Here are some reflection questions you can use with your child to help reinforce the benefits of respect:

- How have you been doing at being respectful lately?
- How do you think I've been doing at being respectful lately?
- How does God tell us to treat each other?
- What happens in our family when we treat one another the way God tells us to?
- What happens in our family when we don't treat one another the way God tells us to?
- How do you think God feels when we treat other people disrespectfully? Why?
- What lesson is God teaching you about how he wants you to treat other people?
- What are some of the good things that happen when you treat other people respectfully?
- What is one thing you can do to act more respectfully in our family?
- What are some things we could all work on to treat each other more respectfully?

Surprise Them with a Reward

Another fun way to remind your kids that respectful behavior is the way to go is to occasionally give them a surprise reward. This is a "now and then" technique, because if you use it too often, it will no longer be a surprise.

If you think your child has been doing a great job with fast listening, flexible thinking, problem solving, or any other respectful behavior, then catch her off guard with a special reward, out of the blue. It doesn't have to be anything expensive. Just the fact that you've noticed her respectful behavior and want to show your appreciation will make it a memorable occasion.

For example, you might gather the children and announce, "Kids, I have something special to tell you. Mom and I have noticed that all of you have been trying really hard to treat each other with respect lately. We really appreciate your efforts and how that helps us have a fun and close family. So because you've been doing such a great job, we decided to take everyone out for a special ice cream snack. Let's go!"

At that moment, your children will be feeling very glad about every effort they've recently made to be respectful. They'll be reminded again that being respectful really does get noticed. And on top of that, there are even surprise rewards! Awesome!

By using surprise rewards and the natural interaction of the circles, you'll find that the respect-privilege connection is a simple and effective way to teach your child one of the relational principles that help us live by God's design. When we treat others the way we want to be treated, many benefits come our way.

You can't force your child to behave with respect. But you can love her, pray for her, spend time with her, teach her the right lessons, let her know when she does a great job—and allow her to experience for herself the respect-privilege connection.

KEY POINTS TO REMEMBER

- Children need to learn that fun privileges are earned by respectful behavior.

- The lesson of the circles is an effective way to illustrate the connection between respectful behavior and privileges.

- To participate in a privilege, our children must follow three steps: start right, stay on right, stop right.

- Having your child rate her "circles" on a 1-10 scale is an effective way to remind her of the respect-privilege connection.

- Reflecting with your child about her choices encourages her to think about the important lessons God is teaching her.

TAKING THE NEXT STEP

1. Read Galatians 6:7-10. How can you apply this principle of sowing and reaping to your child's behavior and its consequences?

2. In what ways does the respect-privilege connection apply to you as an adult, in your relationships or at work?

3. Does your child understand the difference between rights and privileges, or does she seem to think she has a right to fun privileges without being respectful? Why do you think she holds this view?

4. Which of your child's favorite activities or privileges tend to cause conflict? How can you apply the respect-privilege connection to address this situation?

5. How would you describe for your child the benefits of treating other people respectfully?

6. How can the three requirements for engaging in privileges — start right, stay on right, and stop right — be applied to your child's favorite activities?

7. If you consistently apply the respect-privilege connection, what lesson will your children learn?

8. Identify a specific activity or time — while riding in the car, taking your child out to breakfast, bedtime — that will provide you a regular opportunity to reflect with your child about her recent choices. What are some reflection questions you might ask during this discussion?

CHAPTER 8

Use Your Bazooka

the pour-it-on technique

P robability is the science of figuring out how likely something is to occur. In just a few minutes of surfing the Internet, I discovered some interesting probability statistics. For example, the odds of winning a state lottery are about 1 in 80,000,000. And the odds of hitting a hole in one on the golf course are about 1 in 15,000.

On the upside, the probability that a person will be hit by lightning is only about 1 in 240,000. That's encouraging. The probability of getting bitten by a shark is about 1 in 11,000,000. Given the fact that watching *Jaws* as a child made me afraid to get in the bathtub (I still prefer showers to this day), I thought this was pretty good news. In fact, you're about 1,000 times more likely to get bitten by a dog than by a shark. Just to be safe, we have a cat.

And I have even better news: Believe it or not, the odds are extremely high that, sooner or later, our kids will eventually do something they are supposed to do:

- Make their bed.
- Do their homework.
- Put their shoes on.
- Get dressed without a fuss.
- Come in from playing the first time they're called.

The fact is, even the most difficult kids usually make a few respectful choices each day. The problem, of course, is that we're so often focused on the dirt that we completely miss these glimpses of gold. And that's unfortunate, because when a child makes a respectful choice, such as fast listening, a funny thing happens. She thinks something. She probably doesn't realize that she's thinking something, but deep in the nooks and crannies of her busy little brain, your child is always thinking, processing, and evaluating. Some of this takes place consciously and some subconsciously, but it's happening all the time.

So if your child is always thinking, what do you want her to think when she acts respectfully? I figure her mind will go in one of three directions:

a. She'll immediately think about something else.
b. She'll think that being respectful was a stupid thing to do.
c. She'll think that being respectful worked out much better than she thought it would.

If she thinks A, then she's not likely to be aware of the benefits of respectful behavior, and the probability is less than fifty-fifty that she'll act respectfully next time. If she thinks B, then you'll soon have a greater probability of being bitten by a shark than of her being respectful the next time.

But what happens to a child who thinks C? What happens to a child who honestly believes that her choice to be respectful worked out great? Maybe she notices that being respectful made her feel good, brought positive attention, gave her the inner joy that comes from obeying God, or made her "fun circle" go up. Not a bad result for just getting her pajamas on when she was asked to.

This child begins to realize a wonderful truth: The payoff for respectful behavior far outweighs the effort it required. And as soon as your child begins to understand this amazing truth, you won't have to *make* her be respectful — she'll want to do it all on her own.

Are you prepared to see this sort of miraculous change take place in your child? You've already begun the transformation process by setting a respectful example and equipping her with the skills of fast listening, flexible thinking, and problem solving. And through the lesson of the circles, you've begun to help her grasp the respect-privilege connection by showing how her behavior impacts her fun.

Now you're going to unleash the secret weapon for turning on respectful behavior.

Your Secret Weapon

My favorite part of any James Bond movie is watching as the high-tech expert, Q, outfits Bond with the newest and coolest weapons and gadgets just before his mission. From laser beam cuff links to missile-launching sports cars, Bond gets the best gadgets technology has to offer.

Just like Agent 007, you and I have a secret weapon. Of course, we're not fighting egomaniacal villains who want to take over the world; we're fighting the destructive powers of disrespect that want to infiltrate our families. And when we unsheathe our powerful secret weapon, it's like pulling out a bazooka after relying solely on a peashooter. What is this secret weapon? Our positive attention.

Children love parental attention. It's as if any amount of attention, guided by a built-in homing device, sails straight to your child's heart. Wrapped in encouraging words and coupled with warm physical touch, attention from a parent communicates many super-sized, powerful messages to a child:

- "You are valuable."
- "You're an important part of this family."
- "I pay attention to you, even though you think I don't notice."
- "I'm proud of your effort to be respectful."
- "I'm glad God put us in the same family."
- "I love you."

God's Word reminds us that "a word aptly spoken is like apples of gold in settings of silver" (Proverbs 25:11). Motivational leaders, such as Dale Carnegie, Zig Ziglar, Ken Blanchard, and others, have long been aware of the power of positive attention. They revolutionized the business and leadership world with their emphasis on leading through focused, positive motivation instead of hard-nosed, punishment-oriented leadership tactics.

Positive attention, properly given, works wonders in the business world, and it can work wonders with children as well. Just ask Mark and Christine. They sat in my office one Tuesday night describing their personality-plus seven-year-old son. Jeremy was an athletic young boy whose teachers loved his outgoing nature and whose coaches loved his explosive energy in sports. However, when Jeremy walked through the door of his house, he turned into a strong-willed nightmare on wheels. Dr. Jekyll and Mr. Hyde. Whenever Christine mentioned Jeremy's difficult behavior to a friend, the response was always the same: "No, you can't mean Jeremy. He's such a nice boy." While it was not apparent at school or when visiting friends' houses, Jeremy's hours at home were one long series of disrespectful choices, including refusing to obey, throwing tantrums, and even hitting his mother when she tried to take him to time-out.

As Mark and Christine described Jeremy's challenging behavior, the list of parenting books they'd read, and their valiant attempts to curb Jeremy's oppositional habits, I took a deep breath and braced myself for what was starting to sound like a very difficult case.

I met Jeremy the following week and began to teach him about fast listening and the circles of fun and respect. He listened well and seemed interested in learning about how to make his fun circle go up. So far, so good. About two weeks later, I met with Mark and Christine and showed them how to use the pour-it-on technique. Essentially, this technique involves giving a child positive attention whenever he makes a respectful choice, but for optimal success it requires following specific steps, which I'll describe later. Mark and Christine listened intently as

I outlined the steps, and they agreed to give it their best shot (though Christine later told me she was skeptical it would work, which I've heard more than once).

When we met again two weeks later for our next session, Mark grabbed my hand and started shaking it vigorously as if he were pumping for water. "It was amazing!" he exclaimed. "I almost called you the very first night. I couldn't believe it."

Immediately after arriving home from our previous session, Mark and Christine had begun looking for ways to use the pour-it-on technique. Mark saw his first opportunity when Jeremy listened about going up to his room to get his pajamas on. He was surprised to see Jeremy's face light up when he received the pour-it-on praise. Encouraged, Mark watched eagerly for another opportunity, which quickly arose when Jeremy was asked to brush his teeth and promptly obeyed. Again, Mark was taken aback by his son's immediate smile and positive response to the pour-it-on praise.

Energized by Jeremy's positive response, Mark and Christine went gangbusters in following the specific pour-it-on instructions I'd given for responding to their son's respectful behavior. As evidenced by Mark's enthusiastic words on their next visit to my office, they quickly noticed significant progress in Jeremy's fast listening and overall respectful behavior. As a result, the entire family began to enjoy a decrease in frustration and arguments and an increase in family fun.

So let's look at this technique that revolutionized Jeremy's family and can do the same for yours.

Making the Pour-It-On Technique Work for You

Almost every parent I've ever met is familiar with the concept of "praising" children for positive behavior, so I'd guess this is not a new idea for you. Yet your child's disrespectful behavior continues. Why? Because in order to generate the maximum power for behavioral change, your efforts at giving positive attention need to follow three key steps. If you skip any step in the pour-it-on technique, you'll see little, if any, improvement in your child's behavior. But by following all three steps, you'll experience the full power of the bazooka.

Step One:
Identify the Respectful Behavior You Want to Increase

As we learned in chapter 6, most parents are focused on looking for the dirt in their kids' lives. The problem is we've already got plenty of dirt; what we really want to look for is gold.

One way to help move your focus off the dirt is to identify one or two "gold nugget" respectful behaviors you'd like to help bring out in your child. As you might imagine, the most common gold nugget behavior the parents I work with want to focus on is fast listening. Here's a list of ideas to get you started:

- Listening the first time when asked to do something (fast listening)
- Using respectful words and actions when something doesn't go his way
- Using encouraging and positive words with a sibling
- Turning off an electronic activity the first time he's asked
- Going to bed quickly when asked
- Saying, "Good game," even after a loss
- Starting instrument practice without arguing
- Completing homework in a respectful way

The key to success with this step is to be *specific*. Disrespectful behavior often goes unchanged because parents aren't aiming for a specific set of gold nugget behaviors. Like an archer who closes his eyes and just sends his arrow flying in the general direction of the target, their efforts will miss the mark. Any good marksman knows you have to aim carefully and deliberately if you want to hit the bull's-eye.

When you deliberately focus on one or two specific gold nugget behaviors, your child will quickly figure out what respectful behaviors are turning on all the attention — and what he can do to receive more.

Step Two: Watch Carefully for the Respectful Behavior

No matter how challenging your child is, odds are he makes at least a few respectful choices each day. And those are the times you're looking for. They probably happen more often than you think. If you can't find them, then you either need to look harder or redefine your gold nugget behaviors to be more attainable. The more often you catch your child in the middle of a gold nugget behavior, the faster you'll see that behavior increase.

This second step is easy to understand, yet it's the one on which most parents fail to follow through. Why? Because we simply forget to watch for the gold nugget behavior. We're so busy with work, phone calls, shuttling our kids to birthday parties and soccer, mowing the lawn, taking care of the laundry, squeezing in time to cook a meal, cleaning the house, and any of a million other things. Unless we deliberately remain vigilant, our intention to watch carefully for respectful behavior gets buried under the pile of life's louder demands.

Karen, for example, immediately notices when her son Bobby purposely grabs his little sister's toy to make her cry. However, several times every day, Bobby shares a toy or a snack with his sister, or he sits nicely beside her while watching TV. Where's Karen when this is happening? She's busy typing an e-mail, talking on the phone, or catching up on laundry. Bobby's respectful behavior zooms past her like stars in warp speed, and before you know it, Karen has missed another opportunity to pour it on with praise. Karen loves her kids and is a great mom. Like many of us, she just forgets to look for the gold.

The key to success with this step is *high frequency*. An animal trainer doesn't toss his dolphin a fish snack one out of every twenty times it balances a beach ball on its nose. If he did, there would be no dolphin show at Sea World. The trainer reinforces the behavior *every time* it happens, especially in the early stages of training. This helps the dolphin quickly make the connection between the fish snack and balancing the ball. In the same way, if you want the lesson to stick, you must be on the lookout for the times your child displays gold nugget respectful behavior. If you can be aware of 70 to 80 percent of your child's gold nugget behavior, you'll be doing great.

Because this step is so important, I encourage you to find a way to remind yourself to be on the alert. One set of parents I counseled accomplished this by placing Post-it notes all around their house to serve as visual cues to remind them to give their daughter a pour-it-on. After a few weeks, they were remembering to use the pour-it-on technique all on their own.

Step Three: Reward the Respectful Behavior with Focused Positive Attention

In order to get the most impact from your focused attention, you must get in the habit of responding immediately when you notice a gold nugget behavior. This doesn't mean the same day; it means the very instant you see your child act respectfully. You want to make your child so glad he acted respectfully that his head spins around in circles. To do so, you'll respond immediately with two remarkably effective components of attention: *physical touch* and *a specific verbal reward*. When used together, these expressions of approval are a potent combination.

By physical touch, I mean warm, appropriate, usually brief instances of touch. These might include a little hug, a small kiss on the cheek, a gentle ruffling of the hair, or a small squeeze on the shoulders or hand. With rare exceptions, almost everyone loves physical contact, even in small doses. Warm, appropriate physical touch communicates closeness and intimacy, and most kids can't get enough of it.

This type of physical touch is powerful because it is intentional. You aren't absentmindedly bumping into your child because you've misplaced your glasses; you are purposely touching him, connecting with him, and this makes him feel loved, important, and affirmed.

If physical touch is the icing on the cake, then the specific verbal reward is the cake itself. This is where you drive it home. A specific verbal reward simply involves telling your child, in loads of detail, exactly what he did that you liked so much. You want to be extremely specific in your description of the gold nugget behavior you've just observed. You might even repeat his words back to him or run down the whole situation with all the excitement and enthusiasm of John Madden doing the play-by-play of a football game.

The words you choose and the tone of your voice will make the difference between a wildly successful pour-it-on and a dismally ineffective one. For example, if Sam stops playing and gets ready for bed the first time you ask, how would you respond?

Ineffective responses:
- Say nothing.
- Say, "Why can't you do that all the time?"
- Say, "I don't believe it, he actually listened. I think I'm going to faint."
- Say, "Okay, good. Now make sure you brush your teeth properly."

Specific verbal rewards:
- Say, "Hey, buddy, I asked you to get ready for bed, and *bam!* you did it the very first time I asked. Excellent job!"
- Say, "Hey, pal, that was awesome fast listening just now! You said, 'Okay, Dad,' and zipped up the stairs right away, like a rocket. I really appreciate that. Give me five."
- Say, "Sam, thanks for getting ready for bed so quickly, the first time I asked, buddy. You've been doing a great job of fast listening lately, and I sure appreciate it. Man, you're a fast learner."

Can you feel the difference? Which responses will encourage Sam to get ready for bed faster next time?

The key idea is *potency*. The amazing power of a specific verbal reward lies in your detailed, positive description of the gold nugget behavior combined with the big smile on your face and your affirming tone of voice. When you combine that with warm, physical touch, you have a potent one-two punch that immediately creates positive emotions in your child. It's like getting a TV camera close-up just as he catches the winning touchdown in the Super Bowl. Perfect timing. He'll feel noticed, appreciated, and encouraged — and he'll beam from ear to ear. Your immediate and specific verbal reward tells your child *exactly* what to do if he wants more of your positive attention. And we know that he does.

A Tidal Wave of Attention

I've had some parents ask me if the pour-it-on technique might seem insincere to kids who are not used to receiving this much positive attention. That depends on you. Are you using the pour-it-on technique as a way to manipulate your child to behaving better? If so, then I suggest you not even begin. Or are you genuinely thrilled to the core of your being when you see your child choose to behave respectfully? Are you rejoicing in your heart when you see her choose to use fast listening or flexible thinking instead of arguing or throwing a fit? I can honestly think of no more genuine parental response than the pour-it-on technique. When I give one of my boys a pour-it-on, I am thrilled as a father to have a son who chooses to obey God in his daily life by handling a situation respectfully, and I want to make sure he knows it.

To get the best results, how many times should you use the pour-it-on technique each day? I suggest you make it your goal to give your child a minimum of five pour-it-on rewards each day. If you really watch carefully for your child's gold nugget behaviors, you'll find that many days you can give five pour-it-on rewards before she's done with breakfast. This means that you can easily give her five to ten pour-it-on rewards each day. If you do this, all I can say is watch out! You're about to experience a respectful revolution in your family.

Just do the math. Let's say you and your spouse each give your child five pour-it-on rewards each day. Between the two of you, that's a total of ten a day (of course, you could give even more). That's about 70 a week; 140 in two weeks; 300 in a month! And that's just one month! If you maintain the pace, your daughter will receive 1,800 pour-it-on rewards in six months and over 3,600 in a year! And that's only at five a day! Your specific, high-frequency, potent, positive attention will flood over her like a tidal wave. She won't know what hit her.

While you still need to respond to her disrespectful behavior (I'll give you plenty of ideas for how to do that in coming chapters), the pour-it-on technique will help you put more emphasis on her respectful behavior than you ever have before. And what do you imagine your child is thinking when you give her a pour-it-on? Let's see what's going on inside her busy little brain:

- *Wow, where did that come from?*
- *That worked out way better than I expected.*
- *Man, fast listening works out great!*
- *She noticed that? Mom must really be paying close attention to me.*
- *I'm glad I did that. I'll have to do that again.*

When your child begins to realize that respectful behavior is what you're watching for, you'll see the lightbulb go on inside her head. When you really pour on the focused, positive attention, you make it impossible for your child *not* to get the lesson. She'll hear so many specific verbal rewards that they'll become etched in her memory. And better yet, each of the specific verbal rewards was true. She really *was* listening the first time! She *did* share her dessert with her brother! She *did* start her homework without any argument whatsoever! And each time she did it, you gave her a pour-it-on that made her feel like a million bucks.

Some parents ask me if they should use the pour-it-on technique with all their kids. They're concerned that the other children may feel left out if a sibling gets all this positive attention. The fact that these parents are even asking this question shows the powerful impact that positive parental attention has on children.

The answer to their question is a resounding yes! Absolutely use the pour-it-on technique with all your kids. Your whole family will benefit as you let your children know how proud you are of their respectful choices. They'll receive plenty of pour-it-on rewards and see their siblings get the same. You'll create a virtual pour-it-on fest that all your children will love.

In short, you're helping your child find the fun in respectful behavior — and that makes life a lot more fun for your whole family!

- You have a secret weapon for turning on your child's respectful behavior: your positive attention.

- When you deliberately focus on one or two specific gold nugget behaviors, your child will quickly figure out what respectful behaviors are turning on all the attention.

- The more often you catch your child in the middle of a gold nugget behavior, the faster you'll see that behavior increase.

- The combination of physical touch and a specific verbal reward is a bazooka that will make your child feel great about being respectful.

- A minimum of five pour-it-on rewards a day will help your child realize that respectful behavior works out better than he ever imagined.

1. Read Proverbs 12:18, 12:25, 15:4, and 18:21. How does your child respond to your positive and encouraging words? Can you think of a time when your words had an encouraging and life-giving impact on your child?

2. How do you feel when you receive positive attention or feedback from your spouse, your employer, or a friend? Describe a time when you received positive feedback that encouraged you.

3. How many times a day do you currently give verbal praise to your child? In what ways can you improve the effectiveness of your words?

4. Identify two gold nugget behaviors you'd like to see more often from your child.

5. Remembering to watch for your child's respectful behaviors can be the most difficult part of the pour-it-on technique. What will you do to remind yourself to watch for your child's gold nugget behaviors?

6. What form of appropriate physical touch seems to speak most effectively to your child?

7. If you really watch for them, how many gold nugget behaviors do you think you will find on an average day?

8. If you remain consistent with the pour-it-on technique, what impact will it have on your child's respectful behavior? What impact will it have on your family?

CHAPTER 9

Turn On the Juice

behavioral contracts

O n the table in front of me sits a box of Lucky Charms. That's right, the bright red box with the little green-suited leprechaun. Evidently this particular box is rather special because it contains limited-edition double shooting star marshmallows. Right next to the Lucky Charms, a striking orange box of Peanut Butter Crunch, my boys' other favorite cereal, cheerfully proclaims its *super* peanut butter taste. On the back of each box is a fun conglomeration of puzzles, mazes, and "find the hidden cereal bowl" games. We have here the makings of a completely fun, if not particularly nutritious, breakfast.

These cereal boxes bring back fond memories of my Canadian boyhood. I remember eagerly ripping open boxes of Cocoa Puffs, Lucky Charms, and Cocoa Krispies to search for stickers, cool tattoos, and any of a million other small but exciting prizes that lay hidden at the bottom of the box. I'd gulp down my bowls of cereal until I could finally catch a glimpse of the hidden prize peeking out from between the sugar-coated morsels. Regardless of your personal views on the nutritional value of kids' breakfast cereal, you have to admit that the manufacturers have figured out how to keep kids coming back for more. A billion-dollar industry is evidence that they've mastered the art of making cereal fun.

This mirrors what we're trying to accomplish as respect coaches:

using fun to motivate our children to be respectful. We want them to understand that God designed respectful behavior to lead to many benefits, just as surely as I used to find a fun prize at the bottom of my box of Lucky Charms. Feelings of contentment, strong family relationships, increased trust, a high self-esteem, the inner joy of obeying God, a solid character, quality friends, more everyday privileges, and occasional extra privileges are just some of the benefits that respectful choices bring.

Through the respect-privilege connection and the pour-it-on technique, you've already begun to teach your child that turning on respectful behavior turns on the fun. He's beginning to see that by using his fast listening, flexible thinking, and problem-solving skills, he earns more privileges and receives more positive attention than ever before. For many kids, this level of positive reinforcement, given consistently, is powerful enough to teach them that respectful behavior is the way to go.

Sometimes, however, we need just a little more incentive. This is where behavioral contracts come in handy.

A behavioral contract is a detailed agreement that connects a certain positive behavior with a specified reward. Such contracts may be long term with several elements, such as requiring a child to perform certain tasks or exhibit specific behavior over a period of time to earn an allowance. Or the arrangements may be short term with immediate payoffs, such as earning extra video game privileges by practicing an instrument or reading for a specified period of time.

For our purposes, we're going to explore how a behavioral contract, used on a short-term basis, can give you a little extra juice in battling a stubborn behavior problem. For instance, you might use a behavioral contract if your child has difficulty completing his morning routine in a timely manner and you want to give him a little extra motivation to speed things up. Or you could use a behavioral contract to help your child quickly break the habit of arguing about homework.

You might be wondering, *How is this different from a bribe?* When I think of bribery, I think of being paid to do something illegal, such as turn a blind eye while smugglers cross the border with a truck full of contraband material. Or I think of a frazzled mom with a screaming child at the checkout counter, frantically offering the child a candy bar in a last-ditch effort to get him to stop screaming. You will be doing neither of these. Much as a paycheck is a reward for good work habits and an A-plus on a test is a reward for diligent study habits, you are going to create a simple structure to reward your child for making respectful choices.

Using a behavioral contract is kind of like jumping a car battery. Few things are worse than being stuck in a parking lot on a blistering hot day, listening as a sickening "rmmmm, rmmmmmm" sound from your engine announces that you won't be going anywhere soon. You are helpless, totally unable to make your car move, until you recharge the battery.

To get the battery operating again, you pull out the jumper cables to get that little extra bit of juice that makes the difference. Once the battery is charged and the engine is purring once more, you can toss the jumper cables back into the trunk; your need for them was only temporary.

Behavioral contracts work the same way. If your child is stuck in a rut of disrespectful behavior, a behavioral contract may provide just that extra boost of motivation he needs to get moving toward respectful choices. Once the new habit is charged up and running, you can phase out the contract; the pour-it-on technique and respect-privilege connection should be enough to keep things rolling.

Setting Up a Behavioral Contract

Successfully setting up a behavioral contract involves just a few easy steps. Remember, the goal is to clearly connect the desired respectful behavior with a certain reward. You're giving your child a little extra "juice" to help her see that the respectful behavior pays off. You should be able to complete these five steps in about fifteen minutes.

Step 1: Specify the Behavior You Want to Increase

As we've seen earlier, it's essential to have a clear definition of the behavior you want to work on. For instance, you may want to focus on motivating your child to practice fast listening, complete a specific bedtime routine, or finish homework without arguing.

While a long-term contract (such as an allowance) would include several tasks that must be completed, I usually like to start with a short-term contract and help the child work on only one behavior at a time. The behavior needs to be specific and easily observable. This prevents unnecessary confusion and helps the child clearly see the payoff of a particular respectful choice. You can always add other elements to the contract over time.

Step 2: Explain the Contract to Your Child

When you approach your child with the concept of a contract, you'll get a more enthusiastic response if you emphasize the benefit to her. Let her know that you want to help her get better at the particular behavior you've identified (fast listening, doing homework in a respectful way, and so on). Explain why this is important to you, to the family, and to her as an outgrowth of her faith and obedience to God.

Then tell your child that you have a special idea for how she can gain a little extra fun by working hard to improve at this behavior. It's a good idea to state up front that you'll be using this contract for only a little while. This increases her motivation to work hard right away and also sets the stage for when it's time to fade the contract out.

Step 3: Develop a Reward Menu

A reward menu clearly spells out what privileges your child can earn through good behavior. The menu can be as simple as just one item for one positive behavior, or you can provide several options for your child to choose from. If you'd like, the menu can specify a few small items, a few medium items, and one or two grand prizes. How you do the menu is up to you, though I recommend keeping it as simple as possible. The sample reward menu below may give you some ideas.

It's a great idea to invite your child to suggest an activity or privilege she'd like to earn by working hard at the new behavior. The more involved she is in developing the reward menu, the more motivated she'll be to earn the privileges it specifies. Some kids may try to soak this for all it's worth, so don't hesitate to bring your child back into the real world if she asks for things that are too expensive or unrealistic.

Step 4: Explain How the Rewards Are Earned

Menu rewards can be earned in one of two ways: scoring the points or holding on to the points. You can decide which option fits best with the respectful behavior you're focusing on.

Scoring the points involves keeping track of every time your child displays the new respectful behavior. Every time your child displays the target respectful behavior, she scores a point and receives a sticker, chip, coin, or whatever small item you choose for keeping a tally. As your child earns enough points, she can trade them for items on the

REWARD MENU
5 points
Rent movie
Checkers/chess with Dad
Milkshake
15 points
Trip to popcorn shop
Rent video game
Pick Family Night game
30 points
Buy used video game
Take friend to movie
Bowling as a family

reward menu. For example, if you were using the sample reward menu above, when Miranda has earned ten points, she can spend them on a five-point item or save them and collect more to purchase a fifteen- or thirty-point item.

This style of contract works best with target behaviors that are well defined and occur a limited number of times each day, such as:

- Completing homework with good effort and no arguing
- Completing a specified morning or bedtime routine
- Fast listening in a specific situation, such as when asked to empty the dishwasher

Holding on to the points focuses on decreasing a disrespectful behavior and increasing privileges as that behavior diminishes. Using this method, your child begins each day with a certain number of points, represented numerically or with plastic chips. Her job is to avoid losing them through disrespectful behavior.

For instance, let's say our goal is to increase Miranda's fast listening and decrease her slow listening. Miranda will start every day with five points. Each time she demonstrates slow listening by ignoring you or arguing, she loses one point. (As we'll discuss in future chapters, you may want to specify a negative consequence, such as time-out, to accompany this point loss.) Any points Miranda still has at the end of the day go into her "point bank." She can then collect these points to purchase items from her reward menu.

This style of contract works best when the respectful behaviors you'd like to track occur many times a day and are therefore too difficult to track effectively, such as:

- Fast listening in general (points are lost for slow listening)
- Respectful behavior toward siblings (points are lost for treating siblings with disrespect)
- Talking to others respectfully (points are lost for disrespectful communication)

Step 5: Write Up the Contract

Once you've decided on the style of contract you'll be using and have discussed the details, record exactly the arrangements you and your child are committing to. Be sure to specifically note the gold nugget behavior that earns rewards, the items on the reward menu, and whether the points will be earned through scoring them or holding on to them.

TIPS TO SUPERCHARGE YOUR CONTRACT

1. Start with small, achievable goals.
2. Phrase the target behavior in positive terms.
3. Be generous with bonus points for exceptional behavior.
4. Award or remove points immediately when the behavior occurs.
5. Revise menu items occasionally to keep things fun.

Reevaluating the Contract Terms

After you've outlined all your terms, post the behavioral contract on the fridge or someplace where it will regularly remind your child of the benefits of making positive choices and will remind you to watch for those gold nugget behaviors. Be sure to keep up with the points throughout the day. If you wait until the end of the day to give or take away points, you'll lose the impact of an immediate response, and your child will lose motivation to maintain respectful behavior throughout the day.

Review and Adjust as Needed

It's helpful to review your child's progress and the effectiveness of the contract at regular intervals. I find that scheduling an initial review after a one-week trial period generally allows enough time for you both to get a sense of how well the contract is working. In a brief five- to ten-minute session, you can discuss the following questions:

- Have you seen improvement in the target behavior?
- Has your child earned any rewards?
- Does any part of the contract need to be adjusted?

To keep your child's motivation high and help him see a clear benefit to respectful behavior, it's important for him to earn points most days. If this isn't happening, you may need to either adjust your definition of the target behavior (if he's scoring points) or offer more points at the start of each day to be sure he can reasonably expect to retain some (if he's holding on to points).

After you've made any initial adjustments to your contract, follow up every few weeks to consider the same questions. Occasionally you may need to come up with new menu items to keep things interesting. As your child's behavior improves, you can make a corresponding change in the amount of respectful behavior necessary to earn benefits. If your child is scoring points, you'll simply adjust the value of the menu items, requiring more points to purchase the items. If he's holding on to points, you can start with fewer points at the start of the day, prompting him to further limit his negative behavior in order to keep the points.

Phase Out the Contract

When you feel that your child has improved sufficiently and that his respectful behavior is becoming an established habit, you can phase out the contract. Of course, you'll still be using the pour-it-on technique and your child will still experience the benefits of the respect-privilege connection to keep the respectful behavior humming along.

To prepare your child for the change, congratulate him for how well he's learned the desired positive behavior. Point out all the benefits his respectful behavior will continue to bring even without the contract. I like to tell kids that the contract was kind of like lifting weights to get strong. Now that he's stronger at the gold nugget behavior, he doesn't need the contract to help him anymore.

If your child really wants to continue the contract, you can always choose to continue it under simplified terms. For example, you could identify one fun reward that your child can earn if he displays the target behavior for a certain number of days. I once knew a boy who would do almost anything for a pickle. Go figure. So his parents kept a calendar on the refrigerator and marked an X on each day he did a good job of fast listening. For every two Xs earned, he could get an extra pickle for lunch the next day.

Another way of using a simplified contract is to keep a daily record of your child's respectful behavior, using a 1-10 scale (with 10 being best). Define a "respectful day" as a day that receives a rating of seven or higher. Every day your child receives a rating of seven or higher, he earns one X on the calendar. When he has earned three in a row, he receives a special privilege. He can receive additional special privileges by getting four in a row, and then five, and so on.

Keeping Your Eyes on the Goal

Although many children never need a behavioral contract, for others it provides the extra boost of encouragement they need to jump-start improvement in behavior. If you follow the steps I've outlined, I think you'll find that contracts can be a fun way to supercharge your child's motivation to make respectful choices.

Whether or not you use a behavioral contract with your child, remember to continue emphasizing the skills of fast listening, flexible thinking, and problem solving by regularly practicing together. By helping to strengthen your child's respect skills and by using the pour-it-on technique and respect-privilege connection, you're putting together a powerful combination of approaches that will help her learn to honor God and respect others in her relationships. In fact, I think *you* deserve a pour-it-on reward yourself. So from me to you: Great job using these strategies so far. You're teaching your children habits of respect that will shape their lives, and you're showing them the benefits of turning on that respectful behavior. Keep up the good work!

Next we're going to look at how to turn off any lingering remnants of disrespectful behavior.

- A behavioral contract is a detailed agreement that connects a certain positive behavior with a specified reward.

- A reward menu clearly spells out what privileges your child can earn through good behavior.

- Menu rewards can be earned in one of two ways: scoring points or holding on to points.

- It's helpful to review your child's progress and the effectiveness of the contract at regular intervals.

- Continuing to practice respect skills with your child, remind her about the respect-privilege connection, and use the pour-it-on technique will reinforce the benefits of respect that continue even after the contract is phased out.

1. Read Matthew 16:27 and Ephesians 6:8. What do these passages indicate about the rewards of obedience to God?

2. In what ways are we as adults motivated to choose positive behavior in our own lives?

3. Have you ever used a behavioral contract with your child before? Was it a long-term contract, such as an allowance, or a short-term contract? Describe the ways in which it was effective or ineffective.

4. How does a behavioral contract help you reward your child for respectful behavior in a balanced way?

5. Would your child benefit from a behavioral contract right now? If so, what behavior would you focus on, and which style of contract — scoring points or holding on to points — would work the best?

6. What items could you include on the reward menu to keep the expectations reasonable yet make it fun and motivating for your child?

7. Which of the Tips to Supercharge Your Contract on page 123 will be most important for your child?

8. Which of the three tools for turning on respectful behavior — the respect-privilege connection, the pour-it-on technique, or the behavioral contract — will be most effective with your child? Explain your answer.

3

Turn Off Disrespectful Behavior

Love is at the root of all healthy discipline.

FRED ROGERS

The corrections of discipline are the way to life.

PROVERBS 6:23

CHAPTER 10

Caution: Student Driver

keeping them on the right road

Now we come to the question you were asking when you first picked up this book: *When my child acts disrespectfully, what am I supposed to do?* Of course, we've already begun to answer that question, just not in the way you anticipated. Rather than simply adopting new methods of discipline, you've been learning how to train your child to be respectful, which is much more effective in helping him develop self-discipline for the long haul.

We now turn to our final strategy: turning off your child's disrespectful behavior. While negative consequences should never be the primary focus of our parenting efforts, they are an important part of our overall plan. Children must experience for themselves that disrespectful behavior works out bad, fast, every time.

Driving on the Road of Respect

Picture yourself as a driving instructor, with your child as the student driver. Along the road of life, your student will occasionally veer off the road. (Student drivers, you gotta love 'em.) When this happens, your goal as parent and chief driving instructor is to get her back on the right road.

When They Veer Off Course

During driving practice, most students don't immediately slam into a tree; they gradually begin to drift off the road. I've found that disrespectful behavior usually works the same way. It begins gradually and then starts to pick up speed.

Nine-year-old Joshua came home from school one sunny afternoon with one thing on his mind: playing outside, but that nasty little "H-word," homework, stood in his way. Being a reasonable mom, Amy agreed to let her son take advantage of the nice weather. She told Joshua he could play outside for a half hour but that then it would be time to come in and start his homework.

When the thirty minutes of playtime had passed, Amy stepped into the backyard and called for Joshua, who was climbing on the swing set with a friend.

Amy:	Josh, it's been a half hour. It's time to come in and start your homework.
Joshua:	(No answer)
Amy:	Josh, did you hear me? It's time to come in now.
Joshua:	Just a few more minutes.
Amy:	Josh, it's time to come in now. Nathan will have to go home.
Joshua:	Mom, just a few more minutes. We're not done yet!
Amy:	Josh, we agreed to a half hour of playtime. It's over now. You have to start your homework.
Joshua:	(starting to get upset) No, Mom! I'm still playing! I don't want to come in yet.

Did you notice the progression in Joshua's behavior? This is how most disrespectful behavior happens. While occasionally your child may jerk the steering wheel unexpectedly — in other words, suddenly demonstrate disrespect for no clear reason — what you're primarily watching for is a gradual veering off course. By staying alert, you can get your child back on track before he crashes into anything.

And you can generally predict the sort of events that will distract your child from the road of respect. Most disrespectful behavior is prompted by fairly predictable scenarios. Usually it starts with something not going your child's way. Here are a few common ones that tend to bring on disrespectful behavior:

- You ask your child to do something she doesn't want to do. "Please start your homework."
- You ask your child to stop doing something fun. "Please turn off the TV now."
- You tell your child that she cannot do something she wants to do. "No, you can't go to Jenny's house today."

As soon as your child begins to respond disrespectfully, you know it. You can hear it in her choice of words, see the frustration building in her face, and sense the tension rising in her voice. You find yourself repeating the same request over and over. Your child is starting to steer off the road, and she's not likely to correct the situation on her own. She hasn't crashed into a tree just yet, but she is clearly heading in the wrong direction.

Identify the Steering Problem

A child tends to steer toward disrespectful behavior for one of two reasons: either she lacks the key respect skill, or she's just trying to get something good but is going about it the wrong way.

As we've seen, a great number of kids are in the habit of slow listening. Many have complained and argued so often that it's become second nature to them. Like a person who has developed bad fingering habits on the piano, they don't consciously choose a poor technique; it's simply become an automatic response.

Some have turned slow listening into an art form, perfecting it to the point that they've become skilled arguers. Recently I was caught off guard by a ten-year-old boy who sat in my office and boastfully declared, "I'm a great arguer." *It's nice to have a talent*, I thought to myself.

This boy, like many others, was not skilled at fast listening, flexible thinking, or problem solving. Oh sure, most kids can use respectful skills under easy conditions, like when you suggest they go get some ice cream. No problem with fast listening there. But when the going gets tough, their skills falter and the bad habits prevail. The good news is, all that can be changed with a little training and practice.

However, even with the proper skills in place, a child will sometimes turn to disrespectful behavior in trying to get what he wants. And that's where we'll be focusing our efforts in this section.

Sarah recently consulted me about her son's temper tantrums. She told me about an outing the two of them had made to Toys "R" Us in search of a present for Drew to take to another child's birthday party. As they walked down aisle after toy-laden aisle, Drew's eyes grew bigger and bigger. Eventually his little eight-year-old brain lost the battle with temptation.

"Mom, this Batman action figure is awesome! Can I get it?"

Sarah responded as most parents would: "Not today, Drew. Right now we're looking for a birthday present for Ethan."

Not the answer he was angling for. Drew tried again. "C'mon, Mom. It's only one thing. Please!"

"No, Drew. Maybe some other time. Today we're buying a present for Ethan. Do you think he'd like a basketball?"

Nice try, but Drew wasn't taking the bait.

"Mom, you never let me get anything! Why can't I have it?"

Things just went downhill from there. Within sixty seconds, Drew was throwing a full-scale, screaming-at-the-top-of-his-lungs tantrum right there on the floor of Toys "R" Us. Sarah did her best to reason with Drew, even threatening negative consequences if he didn't stop. Nothing worked. She eventually abandoned the quest for a birthday present and dragged Drew out of the store.

As Drew's story illustrates, disrespectful behavior often results from a shortsighted goal: He wants what he wants when he wants it. Drew wasn't trying to lose the privilege of going to his friend's birthday party. He was trying to get something he wanted — a Batman action figure, to be specific. In the back of his mind, he must have thought he had a chance of pulling it off; otherwise he wouldn't have tried. Unfortunately for Drew, his actions completely backfired. As much as she hated to do it, Sarah called and explained the situation to the birthday boy's mom, who completely understood why he wouldn't be attending the party. (If this ever happens to you, it's a nice touch to send a present anyway.) Drew ended up losing the Batman action figure and the birthday party.

Bad deal. Good lesson.

Get Them Back on the Right Road

When your child starts to become disrespectful, you don't have to stand idly by and wait for the inevitable crash. Instead I'm going to show you how to quickly remedy the situation and direct her back to the right road. (If her disrespectful behavior escalates too quickly, such as hitting someone or throwing an object, you may have to move directly to a negative consequence, such as an immediate time-out.)

Suggest the Right Skill

When your child behaves disrespectfully, it's because he's not applying one of the key respect skills you've been practicing together. As your child's respect coach, your first step is to identify the missing skill and remind your child to use it.

Because you've been regularly practicing fast listening, flexible thinking, and problem solving, your reminder will immediately tap into the reservoir of those positive rehearsals in your child's memory. This gives your reminder extra positive power for turning the situation around. All your effort *before* the problem will make your effort *during* the problem much more effective.

So how do you suggest the right skill? When your child begins to act disrespectfully, use a simple question or comment to remind him how to handle the situation respectfully. Here are a few examples:

Situation #1

Your child ignores your request that he turn off his Game Boy and get ready for dinner.

Missing skill: fast listening

Suggest the right skill by saying:

- "Brad, is that fast listening?"
- "You can fast listen or slow listen, Brad. Which do you want to do?"
- "Brad, you can say, 'Okay, Mom,' or ask me a question in a respectful way. Which do you want to do?"

Situation #2

Your child argues when told she must clean her room before going to a friend's house to play.

Missing skill: flexible thinking

Suggest the right skill by saying:

- "Abby, what flexible thought can you use right now?"
- "Abby, what flexible thought from your list will help you handle this the right way?"
- "Remember, Abby, the sooner you start, the sooner you'll be done."

Situation #3

Your child becomes angry about all the homework he has to do today.

Missing skill: problem solving

Suggest the right skill by saying:

- "Will, what's a good idea for how to handle this?"
- "Let's see if we can find a good solution for this, Will."
- "How can we use STAR to solve this problem?"

I have found there are two key elements to successfully reminding your child to put her skills to work. First, it really helps when you suggest the right skill in a calm, respectful way. Your child has been acting disrespectfully for only about five or ten seconds at this point, so you can handle it. This is your chance to show your kids what it looks like when a person is frustrated but chooses to remain respectful (see Ephesians 4:26).

Second, it makes a huge difference when you suggest the right skill as soon as the disrespectful behavior begins. This way you won't give the problem any chance to gather momentum. Also, it's easier for your child to be flexible during the early stages of frustration rather than after her emotions have become intense. I recommend that you suggest the right skill once or twice in a situation. If your child does not respond respectfully, it's time to move on to the next step in getting her back on the right road.

Give Them a Fork in the Road

If your child continues to behave disrespectfully after you've suggested the right skill, it's time for what I call a fork in the road. This simply involves giving your child two clear options and emphasizing his ability to choose.

Picture it this way: Your child is traveling a road that forks in two possible directions. One way leads through a beautiful, scenic route to a lovely picnic spot. The other road quickly leads to a cliff. You want your child to take the picnic route, but as the student driver, he ultimately gets to make the choice. He can choose to be respectful and enjoy a pleasant day, or he can continue his disrespectful behavior and experience the negative consequences. You as the parent will determine what negative consequences best fit the situation, as we'll discuss in the next few chapters. The challenge, particularly for parents who are used to relying on discipline rather than training, is to resist the temptation to immediately lower the boom of consequences. Instead you want to give your child the opportunity to straighten things out so he can experience the benefits of correcting his course.

In my experience, the sooner you lay out the options, the easier it will be for your child to make the right choice. Here's how you present the fork in the road:

First, give a specific description of the respectful behavior you want your child to choose. In other words, tell him exactly what you'd like him to say or do to turn the situation around. Your child has already demonstrated he's not doing his best thinking at the moment, so give him a helping hand. He'll find it easier to make the right choice when your request is clear and specific.

Ineffective: "Jonathan, you'd better start listening right now!"

Effective: "Jonathan, I'd like you to turn off the TV right now, get up, and come over to the table for dinner."

Crystal clear. There's no room for confusion about what Jonathan needs to do to correct the situation.

Second, let your child know what will happen if he continues to behave disrespectfully. In other words, explain where the other road will lead. Tell your child exactly what will happen if he continues to act disrespectfully. You're not trying to blindside him; you want him to be fully aware of the negative consequences of choosing the wrong road. Avoid vague threats, such as, "You'd better start listening right now, or you'll be in big trouble!" Instead be specific:

- "Bryce, please turn the PlayStation off right now, or there will be no TV or PlayStation for the rest of the day."
- "Kayla, I'd like you to pick up your pencil and start your homework right now, or you'll go to time-out."
- "Eric, please chew your food politely with your mouth closed, or I'll have to take your plate away for a couple minutes."
- "Morgan, please pick up your dolls right now, or I'll pick them up and you won't be able to play with them for the rest of the day."
- "Seth, I'd like you to stay in bed and try to go to sleep. If you get out again, you'll have to sit in time-out."

Third, give your child five to seven seconds to decide. Waiting too long after you've laid out the options diminishes the effectiveness of the fork-in-the-road technique. Your child will think he can drag his feet or convince you to give him a few more chances. You can avoid creating new bad habits or reinforcing old ones by closing the window of opportunity after only a brief time.

Fourth, immediately praise the positive choice or administer the negative consequence. After five to seven seconds, it should be very clear what route your child has chosen. If you see an effort to choose the respectful road, then let your child know he made a good choice. He started down the wrong road, but with a little reminder from you, he turned things around just in time. This is progress. If you make him glad he chose the right road, he'll be more likely to do so again.

On the other hand, if he continues to act disrespectfully, then it's time to immediately administer the negative consequence you warned him about. I recommend giving your child only one fork-in-the-road caution in a given situation. This will help him learn that he needs to respond the first time, rather than wait until you have given three or four forks in the road. All in all, the entire fork-in-the-road process should take less than thirty seconds. You point your child toward the right route, describe where the bad route ends, allow him a few seconds to choose, and then be sure he immediately experiences the appropriate result.

Help Your Child Avoid a Crash

Let's look at how you might use both of these tools — suggesting the right skill and giving her a fork in the road — in a real-life situation:

Lisa (Mom):	Stacey, please turn off the TV and come sit down for dinner.
Stacey:	My show's not over yet.
Lisa:	Well, Stacey, dinner's ready now. You can watch TV later. Please turn it off.
Stacey:	(ignores Mom)

Lisa:	(suggests the right skill in a firm tone) Stacey, I'd like you to use fast listening right now, please. Let's go.
Stacey:	Mom, I'm not hungry.
Lisa:	(presents fork in the road) Stacey, I want you to stand up and turn off the TV right now, or I'll turn the TV off and there will be no TV or computer for the rest of the night.
Stacey:	Okay, Mom. I'm coming. (turns off TV and walks to dining table)
Lisa:	That's much better, Stacey. Thank you. You almost lost TV for the whole night just now, do you realize that?
Stacey:	Yeah.
Lisa:	But you didn't. How come?
Stacey:	Because I listened?
Lisa:	That's right. Your slow listening almost wrecked it for you, sweetie, but you turned it around. Good job, that was nice. (gives Stacey a quick hug) Next time, let's do fast listening the first time, okay?
Stacey:	Okay.

Because Lisa responded quickly, Stacey's negative behavior never got a chance to build up steam, and she was able to think clearly enough to turn things around. Then Lisa turned it into a good learning experience for Stacey by pointing out that fast listening always works the best.

Redirect with Problem Solving

Another way to help your child get back on the right road is to use problem solving on the go, as we discussed in chapter 5. This includes the two steps of making an empathetic comment and engaging your child in mutual problem solving.

It's up to you to decide whether the fork-in-the-road technique or problem solving on the go would be best in a particular situation. I recommend that you try both approaches with your child and see which response tends to bring the best result. In many situations, a fork in the road will help your child get back on the right road very effectively. In fact, most kids I know typically respond very well to a fork in the road. However, if your child is particularly strong-willed or has a short temper, you might find yourself using problem solving on the go more often because it gives your child a little more breathing room by engaging him in finding a good solution.

When They Insist on Driving Off the Cliff

The fact is, you can suggest the right skill, give an A-plus fork in the road, or expertly use problem solving on the go, and still your child may argue with you and throw a royal fit. In fact, that's exactly what happens with kids who have deeply ingrained bad habits.

Here's the scenario: You ask Claire to put her coloring book away. She ignores you and continues to color. You suggest fast listening once or twice to no avail. You then give Claire a fork in the road, telling her she can put her crayons away right now and be able to color after dinner or that you'll put them away and coloring is over for the day. Or maybe you try problem solving on the go, asking Claire if she can think of a good idea for what to do next. Despite all your efforts, Claire dramatically proceeds to drape her body over her coloring book in an attempt to guard it against you, the evil marauder plotting to take it away.

What do you do now? As the chief driving instructor, you've done all you can to help your child get back on the right road. If she persists in acting disrespectfully, she's choosing to head straight for the cliff of consequences. In the next three chapters, I'll show you the most effective negative consequences for teaching your kids that disrespectful behavior never pays off.

Meanwhile let me encourage you to hang in there and continue using your *entire* plan of teaching respectful behavior, turning on respectful behavior, and turning off disrespectful behavior. Even if your child's behavior is extremely challenging, the important thing is that you don't give up. When you give in, your child hears the message that if she shouts and argues long and hard enough, her disrespectful behavior will eventually win the day. However, when you use *all* your strategies consistently, they work together to help your child learn the right lessons and turn her behavior around more quickly.

- Most disrespectful behavior happens gradually and then picks up speed. By staying alert, you can get your child back on the right road before he crashes into a tree.

- When your child responds disrespectfully, immediately suggest the right skill.

- A fork in the road gives your child two clear options and emphasizes his ability to choose.

- If you tell your child exactly how to turn the situation around and what will happen if he continues acting disrespectfully, he'll find it easier to get back on the right road.

- When your child chooses the road of respect, make him glad he did so he'll be more likely to choose it again.

1. Read Proverbs 12:18. When you respond to your child's disrespectful behavior, what is your typical emotional level? How can you keep your responses respectful and productive?

2. Read Proverbs 15:1. How might the techniques in this chapter be more effective with your child than repeating yourself over and over, yelling, or grounding him for life?

3. What disrespectful behavior does your child engage in most often?

4. Think back over your interactions with your child this past week. In which situations did your child most often display disrespectful behavior?

5. Which key respect skills does your child need to be reminded of most frequently? Are you regularly practicing those skills together?

6. Does your child's disrespectful behavior tend to happen suddenly or gradually? What are the early indicators that he's moving in the wrong direction?

7. How quickly do you respond to your child's disrespectful behavior? How does it affect your child's choices when you respond quickly?

8. Consider a recent instance when your child veered off the road of respect. How might the outcome have been different if you had suggested the right skill or used the fork-in-the-road technique?

CHAPTER 11

Time to Think of a New Plan

turning up the power of your time-out

I couldn't help but sigh as I watched our fun family afternoon deteriorate into a public meltdown.

We'd spent the early part of that sunny Saturday afternoon enjoying a romp at the park. After two hours of darting through the playground equipment, crawling through the brightly colored plastic tunnels, and sliding down the slides, we decided to go out to dinner before heading home.

As we entered one of our favorite family restaurants, my five-year-old son, Jacob, saw that big red metal monstrosity in the restaurant waiting area. You know, the one with the cool electronic crane that tempts kids into thinking they can actually maneuver it well enough to pick up a cheap stuffed animal or two.

"Oh, Dad! Can I do it, can I do it?" came the inevitable request.

Just what he needs, I thought, *another stuffed animal collecting dust under his bed*. But what I said was, "No, buddy, not today. You already have lots of Beanie Babies at home. Why don't you come sit with me? Our table's almost ready."

"Dad, please. Just this once. I never get to do it." A telltale tremble crept into his pleading voice, and his eyes started to tear up.

I walked over and tried to gently guide Jacob away from the devilish red tempter to the waiting area, where Lora was sitting with Luke on her lap. "Buddy, we've done this before, and it's actually harder than it looks. We're not going to do it today. We can probably do it some other time. Come over here, please, and sit with me."

"No! I want to do it!" Jacob said as he twisted away and ran back to the object of his obsession.

Oh boy. Here it comes, I thought as Jacob started to cry. Lora and I exchanged "What-do-we-do-now?" glances, and I quickly scanned the area for a time-out spot. Jacob was short-circuiting and would probably need some time and space to calm down. Hoping that wouldn't be necessary, I tried again.

"Jacob, I want you to come over here with me," I said as I leaned over to pick him up. "We had a really fun time today at the park. Pal, you have lots of Beanie Babies at home. Remember Derby and Bones? They're your favorites. You'll be able to see them when you get — "

My last-ditch-effort speech was cut short as Jacob hurled the top half of his body toward the red machine as if unable to resist the hypnotic force of the furry little faces calling to him.

More firmly this time, I said, "Jacob, I want you to calm down right now and come sit with me. We are not going to get one of those today. Let's go, or I'll find a place for a time-out."

As soon as the words left my mouth, I knew my fork in the road would have no effect. "No, I want one!" he continued to cry. That's when I knew our fun family time was not exactly heading for a storybook ending.

Jacob was past the point of no return; he needed a time-out in a quiet place to help him calm down and regroup. But where? The waiting room was packed with people. What about our minivan? I consulted with Lora (always a wise move) and, with her approval, carried my crying young son out to the van.

As I slid open the door of the van, I told Jacob, "You're going to do a time-out here in the car. I'll be sitting in the front seat, so I'll be with you. It will be the same as a time-out at home. Quiet feet, quiet hands, quiet mouth. Then you can tell me your new plan, or I can help you think of one. But first you have to show me that you can calm down."

I placed Jacob in his seat and quickly ran around to the driver's seat. As he continued to cry, I looked straight ahead, trying not to give him any attention. In an effort to regain my attention, Jacob started to kick the passenger seat in front of him. "Pal, that will just make your time-out longer," I firmly informed him, "and you'll go to bed early tonight if you keep it up." After another kick or two, he subsided.

Within a few minutes, his crying faded away, giving me an opportunity to offer positive attention. I turned around in my seat and looked at him. "Hey, pal, that's how you do it. You're starting to calm down. Good job. Now we can talk." I put my hand on his knee, and we talked about what had happened. I assured him that we could try a machine like that sometime but that crying and shouting is not the way to make that happen.

I then redirected his attention to the evening ahead. "Do you want to go have something to eat and have a fun night?"

"Yes," he replied with a sniffle.

"Then let's stay calm and go have fun. I get to tell Mom that you did a great job calming down, pal," I said, squeezing him on the shoulder. "She'll be proud of you, and I am too. Are you ready? Let's go."

The Secrets to Effective Time-Outs

As in the scenario with Jacob, time-out can be quite effective with kids between the ages of two and twelve as an immediate negative consequence for almost any disrespectful behavior. [8] (For kids under two, prevention and distraction is usually the order of the day, while for teens, logical consequences and problem solving are the way to go.) The time-out consequence is especially suited for instances in which your child needs a moment to cool down.

Almost every parent I know has tried some version of time-out, but few of them know the secrets to making it work most effectively.

First of all, there are two ways a child can earn a time-out: automatic and gradual. Your child needs to know that certain out-of-bounds behavior, such as hitting a sibling, always will result in an automatic time-out. By comparison, gradual time-out is the result of your child choosing to continue with disrespectful behavior after you've attempted to redirect her through the fork-in-the-road technique from the previous chapter.

Once a child earns a time-out, whether automatic or gradual, you need to immediately follow through, allowing her to connect her negative behavior with the negative consequence. It's important to administer the time-out in a calm, matter-of-fact manner. As you know from the pour-it-on technique, your attention, whether positive or negative, is a powerful reward for your child. Therefore, the less emotionally expressive you are, the more effective your time-out will be. This is much easier to achieve when you respond *quickly* to your child's misbehavior.

Then, to really boost the effectiveness of your time-outs, you can do three simple things ahead of time: choose the right location, teach your child appropriate time-out behavior, and walk through a practice time-out with your child. Let's look at each of these steps more closely.

Choose an Effective Time-Out Spot

The main idea behind time-out is that, when your child displays disrespectful behavior, you immediately remove every possible source of positive reinforcement. This means nothing fun to look at, hear, touch, and so on. To pull this off, you'll find that it's crucial to select a time-out spot that meets three criteria: boring, safe, and easy to monitor.

Every home is different, so it's up to you to find the time-out spot that works best for your family. You also may want to identify a backup location in case two children need a time-out at the same time. It always helps to think ahead.

Time-out spots that often work well include:

- Entryway
- Bottom of stairs
- Top of stairs

- Chair in dining room (or other boring room)
- Mudroom
- Laundry room
- Bathroom

You'll want to remove any items from the time-out area that could be dangerous, such as laundry detergent, if you think your child will get into them. Because the point of a negative consequence is to take away the positives, look around for any items that could be distracting or entertaining, such as shoes or toys, before you use this spot with your child. I've known a few kids who could entertain themselves with a particle of floating dust. If your child can do that, then more power to her. But outside of the occasional dust mote, you'll want to remove anything that could make time-out fun rather than boring.

You can decide whether your child sits on a chair or on the floor and which way she's to face. If possible, position the time-out spot several feet away from a wall to prevent your child from kicking the wall while in time-out. If you're using a room with a door, I'd suggest keeping the door open halfway so you can monitor your child's behavior.

Teach Your Child Appropriate Time-Out Behavior

One reason time-out often fails is that parents—and their children—view it as a punishment rather than an opportunity to help the child calm down and get a fresh start. To help you both experience the true benefits of a time-out, we're going to teach your child appropriate time-out behavior.

Few people know this, but there are two ways of doing a time-out: the short way and the long way. You're going to teach your child the three secrets for doing a short time-out so that she never has to do a long, sad time-out.

Here are the three secrets for a short time-out:

1. Quiet feet
2. Quiet hands
3. Quiet mouth

If your child shows quiet feet, hands, and mouth while she's in time-out, she gets an itsy-bitsy, teeny-weeny time-out that lasts only three minutes. That's right: three minutes. (Aren't you nice?)

Every child I've ever met thinks that a three-minute time-out is a bargain. Don't worry that it's too short a time to prompt a change in your child's choices; a short period of time in an effective time-out spot will bring better results than a longer time in an ineffective time-out spot. The promise of a super short time-out increases your child's motivation to have quiet feet, hands, and mouth. That's the happy part.

The sad part is that for each time your child shows noisy feet, a noisy mouth, or noisy hands, her time-out gets lengthened by one minute. With these additional one-minute increments, the sad time-out can extend up to thirty minutes. It is important to use a timer (such as a kitchen timer or an egg timer) to keep track of the time. You want your child to be able to hear the timer go off when the time-out is done, as this can give her something to focus on during the time-out and adds a sense of consistency to the procedure.

Most kids seem to grasp the concept when I explain that a long time-out can be as long as a whole TV show but that the short time-out is only as long as a commercial.

With younger kids, ages two and three, you can lighten up the time-out by assigning a shorter initial time, say closer to two minutes, and limiting the maximum time-out to fifteen or twenty minutes. Since they can't tell time, just let them know that quiet feet, hands, and mouth will make the time-out shorter and that noisy feet, mouth, and hands will make the time-out longer. That's usually enough information to encourage appropriate behavior.

Whatever her age, your child needs to understand that time-out is a quiet time, not a playing time. It's perfectly okay for her to move hands or feet a bit (especially for kids who are fidgety), but she cannot play with items, bang the wall, kick the floor, and so on. Likewise, time-out is a thinking time, not a talking time. In fact, your child's main job in time-out is to think of a new plan since her old plan (acting disrespectfully) obviously didn't work out too well. She can whisper to herself (to think of flexible thoughts), but time-out is not a time for shouting or talking to Mom or Dad. She can talk to you *after* the time-out is finished.

The key here is that the length of the time-out is not determined by the severity of the original disrespectful behavior. If your child's initial behavior is extremely disrespectful, you can always give her a time-out *and* remove a privilege. However, the length of the time-out is determined only by your child's time-out behavior. This increases your child's motivation to display quiet feet, hands, and mouth — in other words, to exercise self-control and calm down enough to start thinking of a new plan — and we'll take all the motivation we can get.

Here's how I introduced time-out to eight-year-old Zack:

Me:	All right, Zack, today I want to teach you a great new way to do time-out. I think you'll like it.
Zack:	(sounding uncertain) Okay.
Me:	Now, there's a short way to do time-out and a long way to do time-out. If you had to pick, which kind of time-out would you choose?
Zack:	The short one.
Me:	Me too. Well, here's the deal. Most kids don't know this, but there are three secrets for a short time-out, and I'm going to teach them to you right now. If you do these three things, you'll always have a short one and will *never ever* have to do a long, sad time-out. How does that sound?
Zack:	Good.

Once you tell your child about the secrets of quiet feet, hands, and mouth, I highly recommend that you actually sit in the time-out spot and demonstrate the difference between quiet feet and noisy feet, quiet hands and noisy hands, and a quiet mouth and a noisy mouth. I do this in my office when I'm teaching time-out, and kids usually find it rather entertaining.

Walk Your Child Through the Time-Out Process

I've found that it makes a world of difference to hold a short time-out practice so your child knows exactly what to do when the real time comes. All you need is your child, a timer, and a few toys. Be sure your child knows up front that this is only a practice.

Let me walk you through my time-out practice with Zack, which you can adapt to your child.

After I revealed to Zack the three secrets of a short time-out and showed him the difference between quiet feet and noisy feet and so on, I told him we were going to do a practice time-out to make sure he knew exactly how to do it the short way. We chose a pretend time-out spot in my office and threw a couple toys on the floor. Zack was to pretend to play with the toys, and then Andrea, his mother, who was practicing with us, would ask him to put the toys away. Zack's job in this practice session was to refuse by saying, "No way!" Most kids love this part. Andrea repeated her request and, as instructed, Zack still refused to listen.

Zack's mother then gave him a fork in the road: "Zack, I want you to put those toys away in the brown basket right now, or you'll go to time-out." I again instructed Zack to refuse to comply. Andrea now said, "Okay, Zack, because you're not listening, you need to go to time-out." (At this point in your own role playing, it may help to reassure your child that he's not really in trouble; this is just a practice.)

I reminded Zack that when his mom sends him to time-out, the smartest thing he can do is get up and go quickly. If he delays or refuses, he'll lose a major privilege for the whole day, which is much worse than an itsy-bitsy three-minute time-out.

Once Zack was seated in the time-out spot, I asked him to show me noisy feet, hands, and mouth, just for fun. He readily complied with a smile. Then I told him we were going to a mini-time-out for practice. I explained that he was in an Olympic time-out competition and that his mother and I would be judging his performance. He could earn top scores by having quiet feet, quiet hands, and quiet mouth and by using his brain to think of a new plan. Because his old plan was slow listening when his mother asked him to put the toys away, he needed to use his time-out to think of a new plan for what to do when the time-out was over.

Then I called, "Go!" and started the timer on my watch. About twenty seconds into the practice time-out, Zack's mother and I commented out loud on how wonderful he was doing with quiet feet, hands, and mouth. I then reminded Zack to think of a new plan for what to do with the toys still on the floor when his mini-time-out was over. After about ninety seconds, I stopped the timer and told Zack that the time-out was over. Then I asked Zack to show us his new plan. He walked over to Andrea and said, "I'm sorry I didn't put the toys away," and quickly put them back in the basket. Andrea and I gave him a standing ovation.

Practice over. The Olympic judges declared that Zack's time-out performance had scored a perfect ten, so we exchanged a high five. Then we talked briefly about which plan worked better — his old plan (slow listening) or his new plan (fast listening). I wrapped up the practice with a little time-out quiz to make sure Zack clearly understood the main points:

- A short time-out is only _____ minutes long. (three)
- A long time-out can be up to _____ minutes long. (thirty)
- The three secrets of a short time-out are _____. (quiet feet, quiet hands, quiet mouth)
- Your time-out gets longer by _____ (one minute) every time you show _____. (noisy feet, noisy hands, noisy mouth)
- In addition to quiet feet, hands, and mouth, your other time-out job is to use your brain to think of a _____ . (new plan)

Conquering Time-Out Challenges

Even the promise of a short three-minute sentence isn't enough to convince some children to cooperate with the time-out process. I remember Christine, a darling little five-year-old girl with curly blonde hair. Christine's mother assured me that although it was hard to imagine, Christine would regularly kick and scream in time-out for the full half hour. She didn't even get a sore throat. In case you're wondering, we did teach Christine to calm down in time-out, and the last time I saw her, her time-outs had decreased to between three and ten minutes. In Christine's case, this took about seven months of hard work by her parents, even when it looked as though Christine was not going to budge an inch. How did this happen, you ask? Christine's parents stayed consistent with our time-out procedure and used the following ideas for dealing with difficult time-out situations.

When Your Child Refuses to Go to Time-Out

The way I figure it, when your child refuses to go to time-out, she expects you to get fire-breathing mad, grab her by the nearest appendage, and drag her to the time-out dungeon. If this happens, she wins because she was able to push your buttons and pull you into a power struggle.

There's a much better way to handle this situation. Instead of letting it deteriorate into a knock-down-drag-out event suitable for the World Wrestling Federation, quickly and calmly give her a fork in the road: "Melanie, I'm not going to chase you or wrestle you to time-out. Instead I'm going to count to three. By the time I get to three, you need to be heading to time-out, or you'll lose _____ (name a favorite privilege) for the rest of the day. One ... two ... three." When you compare a three-minute time-out with a significant privilege loss for the rest of the day, the privilege loss could be literally hundreds of times worse than the original time-out. Not a good deal, as most children will quickly realize.

If your child heads to time-out after you offer the fork in the road, problem over. If not, inform her that the time-out is now cancelled and instead she has lost that privilege for the entire day. Then calmly turn around and walk away. This is crucial, as it gives your child a chance to think about what has just transpired. At this point, most kids suddenly realize they have just made a very bad deal. They may actually try to bargain to get their time-out back! If this happens, simply explain that her time for choosing is over and that the next time you tell her to go to time-out, she'd better go the first time if she doesn't want this to happen again.

If your child throws another fit at this point (most kids don't), just walk away. If you need to, you can give her a fork in the road between going to her room to calm down or losing another privilege.

For a very young child, aged two or three, explain that he needs to walk to time-out very quickly. If he doesn't, ask your child which he would like to do: walk to time-out on his own, or have a parent walk him there. Emphasize that those are the only two options. Most children would much rather walk to time-out on their own than be escorted by a parent.

When Your Child Chooses Inappropriate Time-Out Behavior

When you send a child to time-out, he has two choices: appropriate time-out behavior or inappropriate time-out behavior. As you saw earlier, we want to encourage appropriate time-out behavior — quiet feet, hands, and mouth — to help him calm down so he can think of a new plan. The penalty for being noisy is one minute for each occurrence of noisy feet, hands, or mouth, up to a total of no more than thirty minutes. Simply tell your child, "Justin, because you are _____ (name the negative behavior), your time-out just got longer by one minute." Then add a minute to the timer.

Once the time-out has lasted approximately thirty minutes, it's time to call it quits. For whatever reason, it's not getting through to your child on this particular occasion. However, this doesn't mean he gets off scot-free; instead he's now earned an additional negative consequence. You can simply inform your child that the time-out is now over. Then, before he bounces off, explain that because he chose not to do his time-out properly, he's lost a favorite privilege — of your choosing, Mom or Dad — for the rest of the day.

When Your Child Acts Up in Public

As Lora and I found during Jacob's restaurant meltdown, it sometimes can be difficult to administer a time-out in a public place. You may have to improvise and, for instance, use your car, a bench at the mall, or a quiet corner at a friend's house. Only use time-out in public if it can be done safely and without embarrassing your child or drawing undue attention. As when I gave Jacob the car time-out, you'll need to stay close by to make sure your child is safe and doesn't think you've left her alone.

If you can't come up with a safe and effective time-out solution, use a different negative consequence or tell your child she will do a time-out immediately when you get home, and then try to get home soon.

When you consistently implement the ideas from this chapter, I think you'll find time-out to be an effective technique for turning off your child's disrespectful behavior and helping him to turn things around by thinking of a new plan.

In the next chapter, we'll see how you can combine time-outs with logical consequences to reinforce the idea that disrespectful behavior always turns off the positives. Your child will quickly realize that respect is the only way to fly.

KEY POINTS TO REMEMBER

- It's important to administer time-out in a calm, matter-of-fact manner.
- An effective time-out spot meets three criteria: boring, safe, and easy to monitor.
- Your child's main job in time-out is to think of a new plan while keeping feet, hands, and mouth quiet.
- It's a good idea to hold a short time-out practice so your child knows exactly what to do when the real time comes.
- Your child will learn to cooperate when extended inappropriate time-out behavior or refusal to go to time-out results in the loss of a favorite privilege.

TAKING THE NEXT STEP

1. Read Psalm 119:59 and Proverbs 14:15. How does time-out help your child learn to give thought to his steps?

2. Have you ever used time-out with your child? How has it worked for you in the past?

3. How is this approach to time-out different than what you've done before?

4. Describe a common circumstance in which you think the time-out consequence will be particularly helpful in changing your child's behavior.

5. Name two locations in your house that meet the three criteria for a good time-out spot.

6. How do you think your child will respond to practicing a time-out? How can you make your practice effective?

7. What are some ways to remind yourself to remain calm throughout the time-out process, even if your child resists the entire time?

8. Take a moment to think about some of the public places you visit often with your family. What options can you think of for administering a time-out in these locations?

CHAPTER 12

When the Fun Goes Down

logical consequences for disrespectful behavior

Gavin is on a mission. It's a beautiful Saturday morning, and he wants to play outside with his friends. He has absolutely no desire to vacuum his room and straighten up the playroom, which his mom has asked him to do. His objective: to get outside as soon as possible with no cleaning involved. His method: to argue, procrastinate, whine — anything that will get his mission accomplished.

True, eight-year-old Gavin probably has not plotted out a plan to the extent I've described, but he *is* trying to get out of cleaning so he can go outside and play. And his arguing is no accident. To borrow a popular term, Gavin's arguing is purpose driven. He's trying to get something good (playing outside), but he's going about it the wrong way.

As we've seen in the previous chapters, the moment Gavin starts to argue, his mother should remind him to use his fast-listening skills and, if needed, give him a fork in the road. If he still doesn't straighten up, it's time for Mom to turn off the positives. Time-out is one effective option. Let me introduce you to another: logical consequences.

The goal of logical consequences is to make a clear connection between a negative consequence and the disrespectful behavior, reinforcing in your child's mind the fact that disrespect will always turn off the positives. This is the not-so-fun application of the respect privilege connection that we discussed in chapter 7. If the respect circle goes down, the fun circle goes right down with it.

Eight-year-old Riley experienced firsthand the power of logical consequences soon after a visit to my office. This precocious young boy had decided he no longer wanted to brush his teeth. He didn't really have a good reason; he just didn't view dental hygiene as a good use of his time. We talked about the importance of listening to Mom and Dad, having fresh breath, and keeping one's teeth healthy and clean. Still Riley remained convinced that brushing was for the birds. It was time for Riley to experience the logical consequences of his choice.

Once more I explained to Riley about the sugary residue left behind by the snacks and sodas that many kids, including him, like to eat and drink. I noted that regular brushing prevents that sugar from remaining on kids' teeth and keeps them healthy. Because Riley's parents love him so much and want him to stay healthy and strong, they wouldn't ever want him to do anything that would hurt his body or his teeth. Therefore, if Riley would not brush, his parents would have no choice but to discontinue all sugary foods and drinks that might harm his teeth. This meant Riley would have to say good-bye to all his favorite breakfast cereals, snack bars, cookies, ice cream, sodas, and so on.

As I described this sugar-deprived scene straight from *A Nightmare on Gingivitis Street*, Riley's eyes grew wide in disbelief. The thought of surviving on carrots and celery sticks was too much for him. No one could force him to brush his teeth, but the logical consequences of his choice were rather persuasive — apparently much more persuasive than all of his parents' attempts at reasoning and nagging. After just one snack-less day, Riley became a devoted tooth brusher.

Logical consequences are most effective when they have a direct connection to the problem behavior, as with removing sugary snacks from our reluctant Riley. As we help our children turn off their disrespectful behavior, we have a number of negative consequences at our disposal. Let's look in detail at some of the most effective options, which can be used separately or in mix-and-match combinations — or even paired with a time-out — depending on what best fits your child and the particular situation.

The Logical Consequence of Privilege Loss

Loss of privileges is the big kahuna of logical consequences. Few things will grab your child's attention more effectively.

As we saw with the respect-privilege connection and the lesson of the circles in chapter 7, your child alone controls her respect circle. But you control the fun circle. And your job is to keep the respect and fun circles connected by allowing her to earn privileges through respectful and responsible behavior and, when necessary, by removing privileges when she demonstrates disrespectful behavior. Privileges include any electronic activity, toy, snack, or activity your kids have or participate in.

Through my work with children and their parents, I've gathered some key ideas for making the most of this negative consequence:

1. *Logically connect the privilege loss to the disrespectful behavior.* For example, if Nicole argues about putting away her Polly Pocket dolls, then you put them away, and she'll lose the privilege of playing with them for the rest of the day, or possibly a couple days. If she colors on the wall with her new markers, she'll get to clean the wall and lose coloring privileges for a few days. In this sense, a time-out is actually a logical consequence as well, because if Nicole is choosing a bad plan, then she logically needs a little time to help her think of a new plan before she gets herself into more trouble.

2. *Adjust the length of privilege loss depending on the situation.* You have several options for how long a privilege loss may last. Generally speaking, here are your three basic choices: less than a day, one day, or more than a day.

The standard approach is to remove the privilege for one day. In general, I define "one day" as the rest of the current day so your child can start fresh the next morning. For a child who usually is respectful, you may want to set a shorter time frame for regaining the privilege, on the condition that he quickly puts those respect skills back to work.

If a child is racking up frequent flyer miles with a pattern of disrespectful behavior connected to a certain activity, then he may need to lose that privilege for a longer period of time. With video games, I affectionately refer to this as a "PlayStation vacation."

I remember when Hannah told me that 80 percent of her arguing was related to turning off the TV. "You've got to be kidding me," I replied. "You mean that if your TV arguing was gone, there would be almost no arguing?"

"That's right," she confirmed, not realizing she'd just sealed her doom.

Before our session was over, I informed Hannah that she would be taking a vacation from TV for the next week. Then her arguing would be down to almost zero. Awesome. Her eyes turned into saucers and her jaw dropped. I think she got the message. Disrespectful TV behavior will make TV go away. For how long? As long as it takes. After Hannah's TV privileges returned a week later, her arguing decreased significantly.

Most of the time, your child can regain a lost privilege only after (1) the specified time period has elapsed, and (2) she has demonstrated overall respectful behavior since the privilege was removed. You'll want to be sure that each of these expectations is clear to your child. For instance, Amanda may lose the privilege of playing with friends after school because she was disrespectful while getting ready for school in the morning. She can see her friends tomorrow if she behaves respectfully the rest of the day and the next morning.

Another option is to allow your child to earn the privilege back early through exceptionally respectful behavior. This option provides powerful motivation when a certain privilege has been lost for several days. You can tell your child that the privilege will be gone for X number of days. "But," you add, "there *might* be a slight chance, if you are extremely respectful, that maybe, just maybe, you can earn the privilege back a bit early." You don't need to give her any guarantees; just planting that seed of hope gives her a little extra motivation to turn things around fast. A word of caution: This option should be used only occasionally, or your child will come to expect that she can always earn privileges back early. Earning a privilege back early should be an occasional exception to the rule.

3. *Combine privilege loss with other negative consequences.* In some instances, you may choose to combine privilege loss with a time-out, another logical consequence, or positive practice (see chapter 13). For example, if your kids are repeatedly being disrespectful to each other and decide to address a conflict with hitting and name calling, they might each earn an immediate time-out *and* be sent to bed thirty minutes early. Or you might follow up time-out with an assignment to write five reasons why it's important to treat family members respectfully.

The Logical Consequence of Early Bedtime

Early bedtime is a simple and effective logical consequence, with the added bonus of giving you an extra few minutes of peace. You can mete out this consequence in time segments of varying lengths, resulting in a bedtime that's ten, fifteen, twenty, or thirty minutes earlier than normal.

When my kids were young, if Lora or I announced that their disrespectful behavior just earned them an earlier bedtime, you'd have thought we just cancelled Christmas for the next five years. To them, going to bed early meant missing out on fun, which was more torturous than nearly any other consequence they could imagine. Since they couldn't tell time, I always got a kick out of the fact that while they might actually be going to bed only five minutes early, we got the same effect as if they'd gone to bed thirty minutes early. All they knew was that playtime ended earlier than normal, and that was enough to help them see that their disrespect had turned off the positives.

This logical consequence sends a clear message: Respectful behavior earns a regular bedtime and a full amount of the day's fun; disrespectful behavior gets you sent to bed early. The underlying idea — which you may even want to tell your child — is that if you find it too hard to treat family members respectfully, then you might as well be in bed getting a good rest so you can have a better day tomorrow. (Parents: No fair doling out unearned early bedtimes just to earn a little extra rest for yourself!)

If a child puts up a fight about an early bedtime, I like to give him the option of either going right to bed or sitting in time-out *and then* going right to bed. After a few minutes in a boring time-out, lying in a warm, comfy bed doesn't seem so bad.

The Logical Consequence of Writing Sentences

If my many years of school have taught me anything, it's that one of the best ways to remember something is to write it down several times, preferably not on the palm of your hand. The act of writing encodes the information into your brain in a stronger way than just passively reading or thinking about the information.

One day Jacob made the mistake of talking disrespectfully to Lora — not a normal occurrence at our house. I found myself wondering, *Instead of just taking privileges away, how can I help him remember to talk respectfully?* Then it dawned on me: writing. But instead of using sentence writing as a punishment, it could serve as a memory enhancer to help him remember to talk respectfully to his mother. It seemed to me that writing fifteen sentences was a lot better than losing a privilege for the day, so I considered it an upgrade. Why not give it a try?

Before we explore this consequence further, let me address a valid concern: I once received a very thoughtful e-mail from a teacher who thought that writing sentences was counterproductive because it teaches kids to dislike writing. As a parent, I certainly understand this concern. However, we can avoid such a problem by implementing a new twist on this tried-and-true logical consequence. If the idea of writing sentences conjures up images of Bart Simpson at school writing, "I will not shoot spit wads," on the chalkboard, let me assure you that's not exactly what I have in mind!

As with the other training tools we've covered, the setup is everything. Here's how you can make this logical consequence a winner:

Tip #1: *Refer to it as a memory enhancer.* The repetition involved in writing sentences is a great way to implant the lesson of treating others respectfully more firmly in your child's brain. Lora and I like to remind our boys that we're choosing this consequence to help them remember to be respectful next time. If they don't remember to be respectful, then they will surely be losing significant privileges in the future. Because we want to help them avoid this sad turn of events, we're taking active steps to help them fix the problem before it happens again.

Tip #2: *Focus on the respectful behavior to remember.* Because the purpose of writing sentences is to help your child remember the respectful behavior he evidently "forgot" to do, you'll want to phrase the sentence in a positive direction. Have him write about the respectful behavior you want him to remember rather than focus on the disrespectful behavior you want to eliminate. For example, instead of "I will not shout at my brother," he would write, "I will talk respectfully to my brother." Instead of "I will not argue with my mom," he would write, "I will use fast listening when Mom talks to me."

Tip #3: *Avoid excessive use.* This tool is most effective as an "every now and then" consequence. When parents overuse it or assign an excessive number of sentences, it leaves your child with a negative impression, which may increase her resistance and actually contribute to an aversion to writing. I suggest limiting the assignment to between ten and twenty-five sentences, depending on the situation.

Tip #4: *Older children can write a short essay instead of sentences.* With children ten and older, another option is for them to write a short essay on the subject at hand. Depending on your child's age, the essay can be as short as four or five sentences or as long as two or three short paragraphs. By making your expectations for the essay simple and clear, you can help your child give some quality thought to the issue, which contributes to an effective learning experience.

For instance, this is a logical consequence I have often recommended when a child has been dishonest or has taken something that didn't belong to him. The negative consequence combination I've used in these situations includes apologizing face-to-face to the offended person and losing the privilege he sought to increase through dishonest means. One boy I know who stole a friend's prized Pokémon card and then lied about doing so had to give the card back, buy his friend a new pack of cards, and then lose the use of his own cards for several weeks. In addition, his parents required him to write a short essay describing several reasons it's important to be honest, which prompted him to give some serious thought to the many reasons God tells us to be honest in our relationships.

After one of my sons treated his brother disrespectfully one day, I instructed him to write four good sentences on why he should treat his brother respectfully. Here's what he wrote:

> 4 good sentences why I should be nice to my brother are, I should because that's what God would want me to do. I think it is loving and caring. I think one very important reason is that it gives me and my brother a better relationship. And because it is also what my parents want me to do.

Now, *those* are some good thoughts to keep his mind busy for a while.

The Logical Consequence of the Response-Cost Effect

As we've seen, many instances of disrespectful behavior occur when a child is trying to get something good but is going about it the wrong way. Therefore, we want our kids to understand that not only will disrespectful behavior never gain them anything, it can also result in their losing something. This is where the response-cost effect comes into play.

The idea behind a response-cost approach is that every disrespectful *response* will *cost* your child a privilege or a portion of a privilege. The response-cost approach is often used with points or chips, as I described in chapter 9. In fact, the "holding on to points" approach to a behavioral contract is actually a response-cost approach. For instance, Joey had a deep-rooted habit of arguing with his father, so Dad explained that Joey would lose ten minutes of electronic privileges each time he argued. If Joey argued three times in a day, he would lose thirty minutes of his allotted electronic privilege time. Because he was only allowed one hour of video games or TV each day to begin with, Joey definitely felt the cost of his disrespectful response. I like this approach because your child knows ahead of time exactly what will happen if he continues to act disrespectfully. No surprises.

You may at times find it helpful to combine a response-cost approach with the time-out consequence, creating what I call a time-out/logical consequence hierarchy. With this system, your child earns additional negative consequences with each time-out he earns during the course of a day. The box below shows the time-out/logical consequence hierarchy I recently developed for seven-year-old Anthony.

Anthony's Time-Out/Logical Consequence Hierarchy

NUMBER OF TIME-OUTS	ADDITIONAL LOGICAL CONSEQUENCES
0	None
1	None
2	None
3	No TV or video games
4	No TV or video games, no outside play
5	No TV or video games, no outside play, no Legos or action figures
6	No TV or video games, no outside play, no Legos or action figures, bedtime thirty minutes earlier

You can choose the negative consequences that work best for your child. For most children, I suggest that additional consequences be added by the second or third time-out earned in a day, because by then it's clear that time-out alone isn't having the desired effect. It's also a good idea to reserve early bedtime for the last consequence on your hierarchy because by the time your child earns five or six time-outs, you'll be ready to call it quits and send him to bed.

The structured predictability of this hierarchy takes all the emotion and guesswork out of the discipline process, which increases its effectiveness. Your child knows exactly what consequences to expect and that they'll grow increasingly worse with each display of disrespectful behavior.

Putting Logical Consequences to Work

You now have the beginning of an effective step-by-step approach to use when your child behaves disrespectfully. You begin by trying to help her get back on the right road. If she persists in being disrespectful, then you can choose whichever negative consequence will teach her the right lesson most effectively. This will usually consist of a time-out, a logical consequence, or both. As always, you want to make sure that *your* words and actions are controlled and respectful.

In the next chapter, I'm going to teach you about one more very effective consequence you can use to turn off your child's disrespectful behavior.

KEY POINTS TO REMEMBER

- The goal of logical consequences is to make a clear connection between misbehavior and a negative consequence, teaching your child that disrespect always turns off the positives.
- To a child, going to bed early means missing out on fun, sending a clear message that disrespect turns off the positives.
- Instead of using sentence writing as a punishment, use it as a memory enhancer to help remind your child to be respectful next time.
- The idea behind a response-cost approach is that every disrespectful response will cost your child a privilege or a portion of a privilege.
- A time-out/logical consequence hierarchy is a great way to emphasize that continued disrespectful behavior turns off the positives.

TAKING THE NEXT STEP

1. Read Hebrews 12:11 and Ephesians 6:4. How do logical consequences help you train and instruct your kids in respectful habits that will produce "a harvest of righteousness and peace"?

2. What logical consequences do we experience as adults? How effective are these at discouraging inappropriate behavior?

3. In the story at the start of this chapter, we saw that Gavin's disrespectful behavior was "purpose driven." What purpose generally drives your child's disrespectful behavior?

4. What logical consequences do you currently use with your child? What changes might help these consequences be more effective?

5. Identify two problem behaviors you want to tackle with logical consequences. Which of the logical consequences covered in this chapter — privilege loss, early bedtime, writing sentences, and response-cost — do you think will work the best with your child? How might you combine two consequences for greater impact?

6. For what recurring problem might a sentence-writing consequence be effective? Would it be more helpful for your child to write sentences (to help with memory) or to compose a short essay (to help her think through the issue)?

7. What area of your child's behavior might improve with a response-cost approach? Do you think this consequence would be more effective if you use a point system, such as a behavioral contract, or if you use everyday privileges?

8. Optional: Try your hand at creating a time-out/logical consequence hierarchy chart in the space provided. How well would this approach work with your child?

Number of Time-Outs	Additional Logical Consequences
0	_____
1	_____
2	_____
3	_____
4	_____
5	_____
6	_____

Let's Try That Again

positive practice for positive behavior

Twelve-year-old Cameron suffered from a mental block when it came to his backpack. Whenever he arrived home after school, he'd walk into the house and, with a sigh of relief, immediately unburden himself of his backpack in the entryway. By abandoning his backpack in the entryway, Cameron was creating a problem for other family members, who had to maneuver around this obstacle when entering or leaving the house.

Repeatedly, Cameron's mother, Terri, had asked him to walk just a few feet farther and place his backpack on a chair in the family room. However, remembering this detail presented too great a challenge for Cameron, exhausted from a grueling day at school, so his backpack always landed in the same place. As a result, Cameron's backpack had become an issue of contention in his family, as Terri explained during a session in my office.

Terri:	Well, I have an issue to discuss. (turning to Cameron) Your backpack.
Me:	His backpack?
Terri:	Yes, his backpack.
Me:	Well, Cameron, why do you think your mom wants to talk about your backpack?

Cameron:	I don't know. (obviously wanting to avoid the subject)
Me:	I guess we'll ask your mom then. Mom?
Terri:	Cameron, I've asked you a hundred times to put your backpack on the chair in the family room instead of just dropping it in the entryway when you come home from school. But every day when you come home, you just plop it down right in everybody's way.
Cameron:	(sounding slightly annoyed) It's not that big of a deal.
Terri:	Yes, it is, because everybody has to step over your huge backpack. It's just not considerate to the other people in your family.
Cameron:	Whatever.

Either Cameron had failed to grasp the concept that his choices were negatively impacting the other people in his family, or he just didn't care. Either way, he clearly needed to have a memorable encounter with a vital truth: Being respectful includes being considerate of others and treating them as you would like to be treated (see Titus 3:2; Luke 6:31).

The answer: positive practice.

Positive Practice Makes Perfect

I love sports analogies, and I thought of the perfect one to use with Cameron as we continued to discuss his backpack situation:

Me:	Cameron, let's pretend there was a little boy who wasn't very good at kicking goals when he played soccer. If he wanted to get better at scoring goals, what would he have to do?
Cameron:	Practice?
Me:	That's right, he'd have to practice. And if he

practiced enough, he'd eventually get better and score more goals. Right?

Cameron: Right.

Me: Well, I think it's the same with you. For some reason, you're having a hard time remembering to put your backpack in the right place. I'm not sure why, but you are. And every time you put your backpack in the wrong place, it causes a problem for other people in your family and gets you in trouble. Have I got this right so far?

Cameron: Yeah.

Me: Cameron, you have six years of school left before you graduate. I'd really hate to see you get in trouble every day because of your backpack. That's hundreds of days. By then, who knows how many privileges you'll have lost. So if you want to get better at remembering to put your backpack in the right place, you need to do what the soccer player would do. And what is that?

Cameron: Practice?

Me: Exactly.

To put it simply, here's the rationale behind positive practice: [9]

If your child is having a hard time doing _____,

then he needs a little more practice at doing _____.

Cameron, for example, was having a hard time remembering to put his backpack on the chair in the family room. He also wasn't making much of an effort to remember, which was disrespectful to the rest of his family. So Cameron needed a little more practice putting his backpack on the chair in the family room. Hard to argue with that.

I've found positive practice to be a surprisingly effective tool for helping kids improve their skills in a wide variety of behaviors, including:

- Brushing teeth
- Getting ready in the morning
- Taking a bath
- Putting items in the right place
- Getting towels into the laundry hamper
- Behaving respectfully in the car

If you find yourself reminding (or nagging) your child repeatedly about the same problem behavior, you're probably more than ready to give your voice a rest and try another approach. So let's look at how you can tap into the power of positive practice with your child and turn a disrespectful situation into an effective learning experience.

Step One: Identify the Positive Behavior You Want to See

As you talk with your child about the areas in which you want see an improvement, it's important to set fair and reasonable expectations and explain them clearly to your child. If appropriate, it's worth the investment of time to show your child exactly what you want her to do. For instance, if you want her to make her bed properly every morning, do it together a few times so you can show her what the bed should look like. No military bed making, please.

Step Two: Practice the Positive Behavior

During free time — when your child would otherwise have been involved in an activity of her own choosing — practice these behaviors five to ten times in a row. The fact that your child is missing out on something she'd rather be doing is the "turning off the positives" aspect of this consequence.

Have your child carry out the entire desired behavior, from start to finish. For some behaviors, such as taking a bath, it may be impractical to actually do the real thing, so you can have your child act out the behavior in an appropriate way. After your child has completed the behavior, have her go back to the beginning and do it again until she's completed the entire process between five and ten times. Do this once a day for three days.

For Cameron's positive practice, his mother had him carry his backpack outside and then walk into the house as he did every day after school. When he entered the house, he was to place his backpack in the designated chair. Cameron repeated this exercise ten times. It took about fifteen minutes. Terri told him he did a great job and that they would practice again tomorrow, same place, same time.

Remember that this is *positive* practice. You don't want to make it feel like a punishment by barking out orders, mentioning that you have better things to do, or reminding your child that it's her disrespectful behavior that has forced you into these practices in the first place. Instead be your child's respect coach and make this a productive respectful behavior exercise.

To keep your practice time upbeat and enjoyable, you can use the pour-it-on technique and assure your child that she's doing a great job. I sometimes use a stopwatch to see how fast the kids can get the behavior done, just to make it fun. They can try to beat their time with each repetition. Making your sessions as encouraging as possible will lessen your child's resistance to practicing and will help her realize how easy this behavior really is. Don't worry about her enjoying it so much that she misses the point; the repetition will make the practice tedious for your child soon enough.

Step Three: Continue Practice As Needed

After three days of positive practice, Cameron had completed roughly thirty backpack drills and seemed to be grasping the importance of putting his backpack where it belonged. At our next session, I returned to the soccer analogy:

Me: Cameron, if the soccer kid practiced his kicking and got so much better that he was making a lot of goals for his team, would he have to practice as much?

Cameron: No.

Me: That's right. Because his practicing helped him get better. From what your mom tells me, you've done a great job with your backpack practice and are doing much better at putting it in the right place. Good for you, pal. So when you come home from school and show your mom that you can put your backpack in the right place in a respectful way, then I don't think you need to practice that day. What do you think?

Cameron: I definitely agree.

Me: Great. But if you come home and drop your backpack right where everyone is going to trip over it, then you're showing your mom that you need to work at looking after your backpack. So on those days you'll have to do your backpack practice. Fair enough?

Cameron: Yeah, I guess that's fair.

Let your child know that this is how it will work. On days when he chooses the respectful or appropriate behavior, practice won't be needed. Super. However, on days that he chooses the disrespectful or inappropriate behavior, he'll need to practice how to do it right.

Optional Step Four: Remove a Privilege Until Positive Practice Is Completed

I've heard of only a handful of times when a child refused to practice with her parents. If this happens to you, resist the temptation to argue with your child. Instead calmly tell her that a certain privilege — whichever one you think will be most effective — has been suspended until she completes her practice. Ask her to let you know when she's ready to practice, and then calmly walk away. If you've removed the right privilege, she'll change her mind fairly soon.

Strategic Response

Positive practice is a great consequence that focuses on practicing a positive skill in a positive way. The negative aspect of this consequence lies in the fact that positive practice takes time away from your child's free time — effectively turning off the positives — and in the somewhat boring nature of the practice repetition. I recommend that you don't overuse positive practice but instead save it for situations in which it's a particularly good fit, such as regular household tasks and responsibilities.

With positive practice added to your inventory of effective options, you now have all the tools you need for an effective step-by-step approach to responding to your child's disrespectful behavior: First, try to help him get back on the right road by suggesting the right skill and then, if needed, giving a fork in the road or using problem solving on the go.

Second, if the child persists in misbehaving, turn off the positives by choosing one or more of the following negative consequences:

- Time-out
- Logical consequences: privilege loss, early bedtime, writing sentences, response-cost
- Positive practice

In the next chapter, I'll show you why it's so important for your child to learn that behaving disrespectfully works out bad, fast, every time.

- If your child has a hard time doing _____, then he needs a little more practice doing _____.

- As with all the techniques in this book, positive practice is most effective when you set fair and reasonable expectations and explain them clearly to your child.

- By keeping the practices positive, you can make this a productive respectful behavior exercise.

- When your child begins to display the desired behavior, the practices can stop — but if she lapses back into doing the bad habit, the practices will start up again.

- Positive practice works best with regular household tasks and responsibilities.

1. Read Proverbs 29:17, Titus 1:8, and Hebrews 12:6. How does the discipline of positive practice reveal your love for your child?

2. What behavior do you find yourself nagging your child about most often? How might positive practice help bring about the desired change?

3. Have vague instructions or unrealistic expectations contributed to any of your conflicts with your child? If so, how can you adjust your approach?

4. What do you think are the most important keys to making positive practice effective?

5. How do you think your child will respond to positive practice?

6. What ideas do you have to keep your practice sessions upbeat and enjoyable, such as challenging your child to beat his own speed record?

7. Review the strategic step-by-step approach summarized on page 175. How is this style of responding to disrespectful behavior different than your typical response?

8. Of all the approaches we've looked at for dealing with disrespectful behavior, which will have the greatest impact on your child and your family? Why?

CHAPTER 14

Bad, Fast, Every Time

responding quickly and consistently
to disrespectful behavior

As we consider how we can best motivate our children to turn on their respectful behavior and turn off disrespectful behavior, let's think for a moment about what motivates adults to do the same. Oh sure, I know we'd all like to believe that as mature, responsible adults, we rarely behave disrespectfully. But let me ask you a few questions:

1. Have you ever broken the speed limit? (These are yes or no questions; no explanations, excuses, or whining, please.)

2. Have you ever gotten a speeding ticket?

3. Would you agree that a speeding ticket is a negative consequence for the misbehavior of speeding?

Here comes the final question. It's a tough one, so in my workshops I usually reward the first person to give the right answer with a king-size Snickers bar (which seems to be an especially popular incentive at women's conferences).

4. Why are speeding tickets relatively ineffective at stopping speeding?

A short pause usually follows this question, and then the answers start coming:

"Because they don't cost enough."

"Because sometimes you can talk your way out of them."

"Because you don't get them too often."

These answers aren't quite right but are good enough to warrant a small consolation package of M&M's, which I toss out from the stage. Finally, a mother whose brain synapses are set on rapid-fire blurts out the correct answer:

"Because you don't get a speeding ticket every time you speed."

Bingo. Say hello to your king-size Snickers bar.

Think about all the times you've exceeded the speed limit, by even four or five miles per hour. You've probably done it already today. When you finish reading this chapter, I'm sure you'll drive down to the police station and turn yourself in, right?

Yet with all of the hundreds of times you've broken the speed limit, how many speeding tickets have you received? One, two, or perhaps not even that many. No wonder you continue speeding. You know that, in all likelihood, you won't get caught. However, let's say the local police come to your house and install a device in the speedometer of your car. Every time you exceed the speed limit by more than three miles per hour, that information is immediately transmitted to a computer at the police station. This computer then generates a ticket, which is automatically sent to you in the mail. No police officers. No red tape. One hundred percent accuracy.

What would happen to your speeding behavior under these conditions, my fellow lawbreaker? Would your speeding behavior increase or decrease? (I think we both know the answer to this.)

And would it decrease slowly or decrease quickly?

I'd say your speeding behavior would decrease fast — greased lightning fast. This supports the idea that a potentially compelling negative consequence can become relatively ineffective because of how it's administered. However, when you change the way the consequence is administered, its effectiveness is restored and you see a corresponding change in behavior.

In this chapter, we're going to look at how this principle of immediate and consistent consequences applies to turning off your child's disrespectful behavior.

A Rapid-Response Parental Unit

If you asked me for one tip for improving the effectiveness of your discipline, I'd encourage you to respond immediately, at the first sign of disrespectful behavior. When I meet a child who has developed a habit of slow listening, arguing, and throwing anger fits, I almost always find that Mom and Dad are responding too slowly to the disrespectful behavior. This is an easy habit to fall into, and we all do it occasionally. Slow responses often occur because we're tired, we're distracted, or we simply give our child too many chances to turn things around.

Here are some ways we might find ourselves responding too slowly:

- Giving Alyssa five minutes to respond to a request when you asked her to do it right away
- Letting Nicholas continue to play his video game after you asked him to turn it off
- Allowing Caroline to continue to argue and negotiate when you don't agree to her request
- Becoming caught up in a disrespectful discussion with Derek that only results in anger, hurt, and misunderstanding

In short, responding slowly means giving your child the signal that his disrespectful behavior just might pay off. Remember, that's what he's hoping for. In the back of his mind, he's hoping he can ignore you, wear you down, beat you in an arguing match, or negotiate his way to a better deal. And every second you allow the disrespectful behavior to continue leads him to believe his chances are still alive.

To exert the greatest possible influence, your response needs to be quick. Not loud or angry — just quick. In fact, you'll notice that the more quickly you respond to your child's disrespectful behavior, the easier it will be to respond in a calm and respectful way.

In responding to disrespectful behavior, you will always do one of two things. In most cases, you will help your kids get back on the right road. You might do this by suggesting the right skill, giving a fork in the road, or using problem solving on the go. But if your child does not correct his behavior or if his initial behavior is extremely disrespectful, such as hitting or using extremely disrespectful language, then your response is to turn off the positives by immediately administering an appropriate negative consequence. The main point here is that whatever your response is, do it quickly.

It can be helpful to remind yourself of your goal. When you ask your child to do something, you want him to use fast listening and say, "Okay, Mom," or "Okay, Dad," and then do it or ask you a respectful question. Depending on the situation, that respectful question could turn into a respectful discussion. If a certain situation doesn't go your child's way, you want him to use problem solving or flexible thinking and respond with respectful words and actions. As my kids get older, I've noticed that their questions and comments are often very intelligent ones, and I would do well to thoughtfully consider them. I may even end up changing my mind about an issue based on our discussion. But the key word that makes it all possible is *respect*.

The power of a rapid response is that you intervene before your frustration, your child's frustration, or the disrespectful behavior builds up too much momentum. It's much easier to turn a car moving at fifteen miles an hour than a car speeding along at sixty miles an hour. When you intervene quickly, you help your child reconsider his choices before his angry emotions start to short-circuit his thinking process.

So how quickly should you respond? I think your response should begin the moment you realize your child is handling a situation in a disrespectful way. That could be within a matter of seconds. When you head the disrespectful behavior off at the pass, you'll be in greater control of yourself and the situation, and you'll be amazed at how much more effective your responses will be.

For instance, let's consider a parent-child exchange that's heading rapidly in the wrong direction:

Mom:	Devin, since a commercial is on, would you please take out the garbage for me?
Devin:	In a little bit.
Mom:	Devin, I'd like you to do it now, please. It won't take long.
Devin:	I'm not finished with my show. I'll do it later.

Just ten seconds into this conversation, it's crystal clear that Devin has chosen not to use fast listening. Did he say, "Okay, Mom"? Nope. Did he ask a question in a respectful way? Nope. Then he is choosing to use slow listening, which is not an appropriate response. As soon as Mom realizes Devin is choosing to be disrespectful, her response should be to immediately suggest the right skill, provide a fork in the road, or use problem solving on the go if needed. Then, if Devin persists in responding disrespectfully, she should administer a negative consequence.

Mom:	Devin, I'd like you to use fast listening, please. (reminding him to use the right skill)
Devin:	(ignores her)
Mom:	Devin, I'd like you to take the garbage out right now, please, or we'll turn the TV off for the rest of the day. (giving him a fork in the road)
Devin:	Mom, can I please do it later? (asking a question in a respectful way)
Mom:	It would really help me if you'd take it out now, otherwise the TV is off. It's up to you.
Devin:	Okay, Mom.

Devin pushed this situation to the edge but ultimately decided that taking the garbage out was better than losing TV privileges. His story highlights the fact that a quick response creates a winning situation in several ways:

- Your frustration hasn't had time to build, so your response is more controlled and respectful.
- Your child's frustration hasn't had time to build, so he has a better chance of getting back on the right road and avoiding a negative consequence.
- Over time, your child will come to expect a quick response from you, which will reduce his motivation to try the disrespectful behavior in the first place.

The Persuasive Power of Consistency

While driving home from work one night, I suddenly noticed red lights flashing in my rearview mirror. I slowed down a little to let the patrol car pass. But when I heard the siren and realized he was staying right on my bumper, I realized those flashing lights were meant for me. I'd been driving thirteen miles above the speed limit, and the officer handed me a seventy-five-dollar ticket as a memento of the occasion.

As if that weren't bad enough, less than three months later I got nailed again for speeding in the very same place—I mean the exact same city block. I couldn't believe it! I felt like the victim of a bad practical joke. The officer's car had been parked in the exact same location. Again, I had been driving thirteen miles above the speed limit, and again I was given a seventy-five-dollar ticket to highlight the experience in my memory. Unbelievable.

After my second ticket, a funny thing happened: I started to slow down *before* I reached that dreaded spot on my drive home. In fact, I carefully watched my speed from the very second I left my office parking lot. I didn't care who passed me; let them buzz along like flies headed toward a spiderweb. I was not going to exceed thirty-five miles per hour.

One ticket didn't change my behavior. Two tickets in the same spot did. Why? Because the first ticket could have been a random event. But two tickets in a row? At the exact same location? Coincidence? I think not.

The second ticket made the officer's behavior predictable. Now I knew that the officer would be at this spot frequently. His consistency prompted me to expect him to be there, and I was able to change my driving behavior well in advance. I can assure you that even as I drive home tonight on that same stretch of road, I'll be aware of my speed and will stay well within the speed limit (in case any police officers are reading this!).

The connection between this story and our efforts to turn off our children's disrespectful behavior should be obvious. You've heard a thousand times that it's important for parents to be consistent. But do you know why? Because consistency results in predictability. When an event is predictable, it can enter into your child's decision-making process *before* he acts and will potentially affect his behavior.

You want your child to learn that disrespectful behavior works out bad, fast, *every time*. Not bad, fast, sometimes, or bad, fast, but only when Mom gets mad enough. Bad, fast, every time.

If your child thinks that one-third of the time his misbehavior works out bad, one-third of the time no one notices, and one-third of the time it works out good, then that means that two-thirds of the time, his disrespectful behavior works out neutral or better. Those are better odds than you'll ever get in Vegas! He'll continue engaging in disrespectful behavior — you can count on it.

However, if his experience teaches him that disrespectful behavior works out bad, fast, every single time he does it, then he's going to quickly figure out that it's not such a good idea. He'll anticipate that disrespectful behavior will work out bad *before* he does it.

The Right Lesson at the Right Time

I realize that this emphasis on quickly and consistently dealing with your child's disrespectful behavior might sound rather strict, especially if you're trying to teach your child about showing grace to others. Of course, it's always your judgment call as to how best to teach your child the right lesson in a particular situation. If your child is sincerely repentant and seems to have truly grasped the idea that her behavior needs to change, you have the prerogative to lighten or even forgo a negative consequence on occasion. A genuine apology may be consequence enough in some situations and for some children. However, most often this will be the exception, not the rule. An appropriate negative consequence, even a light one, usually plays a vital part in helping your child learn the right lesson about treating others respectfully.

Let me put it this way: If you fed a dollar into a vending machine and it took your dollar without giving you any food, what would you do? You might try again. What would you do if it gobbled up your dollar a second time, with nothing to show for it? I'm pretty sure you wouldn't be putting a third dollar in that machine. Why? Because it's working out bad, fast, every time. As soon as you realized that machine is a rip-off, you'd stop putting your hard-earned money into it.

In the same way, you want your child to learn to invest her energy in behavior that pays off in healthy, satisfying relationships. For this to happen, she needs to learn that disrespectful behavior, like any kind of disobedience against God, is always a rip-off. It works out bad, fast, every time.

While no parent can be consistent 100 percent of the time, when you do your best to respond quickly and consistently to your child's disrespectful behavior, you will help her learn that disrespect doesn't pay off. This will motivate her to avoid hurtful behavior and instead develop the lasting habit of obeying God in her daily relationships.

- The effectiveness of a potentially compelling negative consequence depends on how it's administered.

- Responding slowly means giving your child the signal that his disrespectful behavior just might pay off.

- The power of a quick response is that you intervene before your frustration, your child's frustration, or the disrespectful behavior builds up too much momentum.

- You want your child to learn that disrespectful behavior works out bad, fast, every time.

- When your child comes to expect a quick response from you, it will reduce his motivation to try the disrespectful behavior in the first place.

1. Read Proverbs 22:6 and Hebrews 12:1. When do you find it most difficult to persevere in the task of training your children?

2. Read Proverbs 15:23. Why is a quick response such an important part of your approach to reducing your child's disrespectful behavior? What message does your child hear when your response is usually slow?

3. Have you ever received a speeding ticket? In what way, if any, did it change your driving behavior?

4. In what other situations do we adults tend to push the envelope, believing we have little chance of being caught?

5. On a scale of 1 to 10, with 10 being "ultra-efficient," how would you rate the consistency and speed of your responses to your child's disrespectful behavior? Under what circumstances do you tend to respond too slowly?

6. When you don't respond firmly and rapidly to your child's disrespectful behavior, what happens to your own emotions? To his attitude?

7. How do you decide when to give a negative consequence to your child and when to let a discussion and apology be sufficient?

8. Over time, what impact will responding quickly and consistently have on your child's behavior?

CHAPTER 15

Call Off the SWAT Team

the bottom line on spanking

I n all of this discussion of logical consequences and the most effective means of turning off a child's disrespectful behavior, you may have noticed that spanking hasn't come up before this. Since I didn't include any form of corporal punishment in my list of effective negative consequences, you may suspect that I'm not an avid fan of spanking.

The fact is, spanking remains a controversial discipline technique, with opinions on the subject varying widely within both the Christian and secular communities. So what does the Bible, our ultimate parenting manual, say about this issue?

In Scripture, we find many passages that refer to the importance of discipline (see Proverbs 6:23; 10:17), proverbial references to physical punishment (see Proverbs 22:15; 23:13-14), and various words translated as "discipline" and for which the concept of physical correction is one of the possible meanings, along with training, instruction, and verbal correction (see Proverbs 13:24; Hebrews 12:7-11).

However, it's important to note that not once does the Bible *command* us to spank our children. We are commanded to discipline them, yes, but this does not mean we must use corporal punishment. In other words, if you decide you don't want to spank your kids, you don't have to.

On the other hand, giving a child a mild, appropriate spanking is never *forbidden* in Scripture. Therefore, I must conclude that if a mild spanking is neither commanded nor forbidden by Scripture, then it is *allowed* by Scripture.

So how can you determine whether or not spanking is the right choice for your family? Rather than a once-and-for-all "yes" or "no," the answer actually may be "sometimes."

To Spank or Not to Spank

Since we've established that spanking is allowed by Scripture, the next question is how and when it should be used. Just because a play is in the playbook doesn't mean you have to use it every game. In football, for example, many plays are used frequently, other plays are pulled out only rarely, and some coaches will choose not to use certain plays at all.

One reason the issue of spanking has become such a hot-button topic is that we all long for a quick fix. We want to know that if we follow a particular approach to parenting and discipline, our children will, without fail, turn out to be responsible, productive, enjoyable, successful adults. Some spanking advocates promote this form of discipline as the silver bullet that will defeat all kinds of behavioral problems.

The truth is that usually there is no quick fix and that no silver bullet solution can substitute for years of careful training, teaching, and relationship building. In fact, spanking can potentially result in several serious negative side effects if it's used either too frequently or with excessive force:

- Spanking can become physically abusive.
- Spanking can severely damage the parent-child relationship.
- Spanking can teach a child that aggression is a valid way to solve problems.

- Spanking fails to teach social lessons that apply outside the home.
- When spanking is the primary negative consequence, the negative behavior tends to resurface when the threat of spanking is removed.

Given the concerns I've noted, you may be surprised to learn that both Lora and I spanked our kids when they were younger. While we used this form of discipline only a handful of times, it was almost always to correct behavior that could have brought harm to our kids, such as running toward the street, or that was significantly disrespectful, such as refusing to go to time-out. While we could have used other approaches in any of these situations, we were both open to the possibility that a mild spanking could help teach our boys the right lesson. Within the context of a loving relationship, a mild spanking can serve as an immediate deterrent and can help impress a certain boundary in a child's memory. However, while we sometimes spanked our kids, our main approach was to practice respectful behavior, use the pour-it-on technique, include an occasional behavioral contract, and apply negative consequences such as time-out, privilege loss, and early bedtime.

Speaking for myself, I chose to limit my use of spanking for very specific reasons. First, I realized that spanking could easily become a reflexive act of frustration on my part. Not every spanking was the result of knee-jerk frustration, but a few were, and I could see how easy it was for me to fall into this trap. I've found the same to be true of shouting. These aren't the ways I wanted to teach my kids the right lessons.

Second, I realized that spanking did not teach my kids the type of social lessons that apply to situations outside the home. In the mind of a four-year-old child, the lesson of spanking is that if you act in a certain way, you could get a spanking on your bottom. While this may provide a temporary deterrent, it's not a widely applicable lesson, because no one else is going to spank your kids (nor should they). Over time I found that I much preferred the respect-privilege connection, which teaches that disrespectful behavior can make any number of their privileges decrease. This lesson is effective and logical and fits nicely with the real-life lessons they experience at school, with other adults, with friends, on sports teams, and so on.

Third, I was convinced that if I put a little thought into it, I could think of an approach that would teach my boys the right lessons more effectively than a few whacks on the rear end would. The result of that line of reasoning has led me to the three strategies I've shared with you in this book. A mild spanking may be useful on occasion to help impress a certain boundary in a child's mind, but by and large I'm absolutely convinced that taking the time to teach respectful behavior, turn on respectful behavior, and turn off disrespectful behavior (with time-out, logical consequences, and positive practice) is the most effective way to teach our kids to be respectful.

Trying Another Way

Many parents have told me that they've spanked their child countless times and that yet the disrespectful behavior continued. As these same parents learned the strategies presented in this book, they experienced much greater changes in their child's behavior than ever before.

I remember my first meeting with Steve and Shelly, whose five-year-old son, Cody, gave new meaning to the phrase "strong-willed child." They came to me because they'd run out of ideas for dealing with his challenging behavior, which included talking back, arguing, and refusing to do what they asked.

These concerned parents had tried everything they knew of to turn their young son around. Like many parents of strong-willed kids, they'd tried spanking many times but found that it only inflamed his anger and often escalated an already difficult situation. "I think spanking just makes him madder," Shelly told me during one session.

I advised Steve and Shelly to stop spanking Cody, as it was clearly counterproductive. We shifted their focus from discipline to training, just as we've been doing throughout this book. I taught Cody about fast listening and the fun and respect circles. Steve and Shelly began daily fast-listening practices at home. Cody quickly caught on to the connection between his fun and respect circles. He showed an initial improvement in fast listening, which greatly encouraged his parents.

However, the honeymoon soon came to an end, and Cody slipped back into his slow listening habits. This is not unusual during the initial phase of teaching respectful behavior. As they continued their fast listening practices over the next couple of months, Steve and Shelly began to combine that with the other approaches they were learning, including using the pour-it-on technique, suggesting the right skill, offering a fork in the road, implementing a more effective time-out procedure, and applying a behavioral contract.

The behavioral contract we used with Cody was relatively simple but extremely effective. Each day's overall behavior was summarized by either a happy face or a sad face. If Cody had demonstrated fast listening for most of the day, a happy face was marked on the calendar, located on the refrigerator door. If he had a slow listening day, his parents drew a sad face on the calendar. Cody and his parents made a short list of rewards he would receive if he earned a certain number of happy faces each week. His first goal was to earn three happy faces, which he accomplished in the first week. His reward was a trip to the local popcorn shop. Cody was ecstatic. His next goal was to earn four happy faces, for which he received a small Lego toy. The goal after that was five happy faces, and so on.

Like many parents, Steve and Shelly were surprised by the obvious improvement in Cody's attitude and behavior when they turned on their bazooka and gave him specific, positive attention with the pour-it-on technique. To their great relief, Cody quickly responded to their new time-out procedure as well. With the incentive of receiving a shorter time-out for quiet feet, hands, and mouth, he received only a handful of time-outs that were longer than twenty minutes. Within a month, most of Cody's time-outs lasted ten minutes or less, and they were growing shorter each week.

Cody's behavioral improvement took a lot of hard work and persistence from both him and his parents. He had good weeks and bad weeks, and sometimes Steve and Shelly felt worn out and discouraged. But they stuck with our three strategies — teach respectful behavior, turn on respectful behavior, and turn off disrespectful behavior — and over time, Cody's behavior improved significantly.

The point I want to emphasize is that spanking was not a necessary ingredient for resolving Cody's difficult behavior.

The Bottom Line (No Pun Intended)

When all is said and done, the decision to spank or not to spank lies with each individual family. If you decide not to include spanking as a negative consequence in your family, you are well equipped to raise respectful kids with the approaches you've learned in this book. However, if you decide to occasionally use a mild spanking as a consequence, then I strongly recommend the following spanking guidelines:

- Only with kids between the ages of two and five years old (Prevention and distraction are the best responses for kids younger than two, and kids older than five are increasingly able to understand the logical connection between their behavior and various logical consequences.)
- On the buttocks
- Over the clothes
- With an open hand (so you can feel how hard you're spanking)
- No more than two to three swats
- Never hard enough to leave welts, bruises, or red marks, or to injure a child in any way
- Used infrequently (Rely mainly on the approaches you've learned in this book, even with kids between two and five years old.)

Let me repeat that the choice to use spanking excessively, either in frequency or severity, is never appropriate and can constitute abusive behavior toward your child.

At the risk of oversimplifying, let me divide the kids I've seen into two general groups: easy kids and difficult kids. Let's start with the difficult kids. These are your strong-willed, difficult-temperament variety, such as Cody. In my experience, these are the kids who when spanked will look you straight in the eye and ask, "Is that all you've got?" Needless to say, spanking is not an effective approach with these kids.

Now let's talk about the easier kids. They can still be disrespectful, to be sure, but they're generally easier to manage. They will respond to a mild spanking and will usually make an effort to avoid spankings in the future. But these kids will also respond well to all the techniques you've learned in this book. With these kids, spanking is typically not needed because you can get great results with the other approaches.

I encourage you to keep your eyes focused on your goal of bringing out the best in your child. As you become increasingly skilled with our three core strategies — teach respectful behavior, turn on respectful behavior, and turn off disrespectful behavior — I believe you'll find them to be the most effective approach for teaching your child to respond to life's challenges in a respectful way.

- A mild, appropriate spanking is neither forbidden nor commanded by Scripture. Therefore, it is allowed — but not required — as a negative consequence option.

- Spanking excessively, either in frequency or severity, is never appropriate and can constitute abusive behavior toward your child.

- Within the context of a loving relationship, a mild, appropriate spanking can serve as an immediate deterrent and can help impress a certain boundary in a child's memory.

- Spanking should never become your primary method of discipline.

- If you decide not to use spanking as a negative consequence, you are well equipped to raise respectful kids with the approaches you've learned in this book.

1. Take a look at Proverbs 6:23, Proverbs 13:24, Ephesians 6:4, Hebrews 12:11, and James 1:19. How do these verses shape your view of spanking as a method for teaching respectful behavior?

2. Describe some of the conflicting opinions you've read or heard about on both sides of the spanking issue. What evidence supports each side's position?

3. Was spanking used in your family when you were a child? If so, how did it affect your behavior?

4. Have you ever spanked one of your children? How effective was spanking in reducing the negative behavior?

5. Would you describe your child as an easy or difficult child? Why?

6. If you have spanked your child, can you think of another approach you could have taken in that situation? Would the other approach have been more effective? Explain.

7. What lesson does spanking teach your child? How well does this lesson apply to situations outside the home (school, friends, activities)?

8. If you decide to spank your child, how can you safeguard against spanking in an excessive or abusive way?

CHAPTER 16

A Demolition Expert or a Gardener

smashing through problems versus
nurturing a relationship

When I first met eleven-year-old Katie, I was struck by how much anger radiated from this talented young girl. Katie earned As and Bs at school, had nice girlfriends, and played on the basketball team. Despite these positive areas of her life, she displayed a hair-trigger temper at home, and most of her anger was aimed at Sherri, her mother. The moment Sherri made a request that her daughter didn't like, Katie would start to lose it.

"I hate you!"

"Why are you trying to wreck my life?"

"Just leave me alone!"

As I talked with Katie about her angry feelings, a larger picture began to unfold. I asked Katie why she wasn't angry at Patrick, her dad. After all, he asked her to do things too. As we talked, Katie described a more balanced and affectionate relationship with her dad. She felt that her dad listened to her and understood her. In fact, he often became the peacemaker when Katie and Sherri battled. It was a different story when Katie described her relationship with her mother. "All she does is nag me," she complained.

"She's always putting me down. It's as if nothing I do is ever good enough for her. I get so sick of it that I don't even want to be around her."

Sherri's style of training her daughter was tearing their relationship apart.

Your Training Style

The Scripture that has provided the foundation for this book is Proverbs 22:6, which tells us to train our children in the way they should go, and when they are old they will not turn from it. We have focused on one particular part of that training: teaching our children to be respectful. As Katie's relationship with her parents demonstrates, we all have different personalities and will have different styles of training and coaching as well. But we need to be aware of how our style of training may be impacting our child in unintended ways and possibly undermining our efforts to instill respect.

As this book draws to a close, I'd like you to think about your training style for a moment. Speaking in broad strokes, you can train your child in one of two basic ways: like a demolition expert or like a gardener.

Training Your Child Like a Demolition Expert

When your child misbehaves, you can attempt to wipe out her disrespectful behavior like a demolition expert. You can bring in your sledgehammer and wrecking ball and start smashing away with angry words and harsh responses fueled by your frustration. I've seen moms come down on their kids like a five-hundred-pound wrecking ball, and I've seen dads do it too: shouting, hurtful comments, voices sharp with obvious disgust. I suspect that at one time or another, we've all responded to our kids' disrespectful behavior like a demolition expert.

If you've ever seen a demolition crew at work tearing down a building, you know they have one objective: to destroy the building. Their job is to knock that building to the ground, and they are usually pretty proficient at doing just that.

While you obviously do not have the objective of destroying your child or your family, the fact remains that if you train your child like a demolition expert, then sooner or later, your destructive anger will take its toll. It will tear her down on the inside and begin to destroy your relationship with the child who once was a little baby in your arms. You'll bruise the tender heart that God has entrusted to your care and wreak havoc on her fragile self-esteem. Once the damage is done, you may spend weeks, months, or even years trying to rebuild your relationship — and it may never be quite the same again.

I remember listening with unspeakable sadness as sixteen-year-old Tim sat in my office and told me he couldn't wait for the day he could press the eject button and escape his family for good. I can tell you with certainty that Tim's relationship with his parents didn't start out damaged sixteen years ago when his mother first looked into his eyes and held him in her arms. The damage occurred gradually, through hundreds of hurtful, disrespectful interactions between Tim and his parents.

Parents certainly are not always to blame for damaged relationships, but trying to train a child with a demolition-like approach certainly doesn't lead to healing. Where would any of us be if God trained us like a demolition expert? With all the mistakes I make, I know my building wouldn't stand a chance.

Training Your Child Like a Gardener

Your child doesn't want you to train her like a demolition expert. And that's not the style God models for us, either. Instead we're called to train our children like a gardener. What does a gardener do? A gardener plants some seeds, waters those seeds so they grow, and then removes any weeds that are left over, being careful not to damage his flowers as he does so.

How does that apply to raising respectful kids?

First, you plant the seeds of respectful behavior skills by leading through example and teaching your child how to fast listen, use flexible thoughts, and solve problems in a respectful way. These are skills that will teach her to honor God in her everyday relationships and respond creatively and effectively to life's challenges.

Second, you use the respect-privilege connection and the pour-it-on technique to water those newfound respect skills. Perhaps you add a behavioral contract now and then to encourage faster growth. You help your child experience the awesome benefits of obeying God by treating others the way she would like to be treated. You teach her to find joy in considering others ahead of herself, to notice how smoothly things go when she communicates with love and kindness, and to reap the rewards of respectful behavior.

Finally, you carefully pull out the weeds: your child's bad habits. But as you do so, you take great care to make sure you don't damage the roots of your relationship or the new blooms of respectful behavior. You temper your discipline style with respect and love, always striving to teach your child the right lessons, the right way. You guard and protect your flowers, knowing they're God's precious gift to you.

When you train your child like a gardener, wonderful things begin to happen. New respectful behaviors begin to take root and grow into habits that will shape her character and bless her future. Your kids' sibling relationships have a chance to grow closer because it's much easier to like and be kind to someone who treats you respectfully. Your entire family experiences the benefits of respectful communication and of learning to work out family problems in a respectful way.

From Wrecking Crew to Master Gardener

When I talked with Patrick and Sherri, I soon realized that Katie's description of her family was pretty accurate. Somewhere along the way, Sherri had turned into the disciplinarian of the family. She was the "bad cop" and Patrick was the "good cop." With refreshing honesty, Sherri admitted that she often nagged and yelled at Katie, though she hated to hear herself do it. Without realizing it, Sherri had begun to train Katie like a demolition expert. The good news was, she wanted to become a gardener.

We took a look at the "good cop, bad cop" pattern she and Patrick had fallen into and decided that it was causing both of them to over-compensate for the other in harmful ways: Patrick was more lenient because of Sherri's strictness, and Sherri was more strict because of Patrick's leniency.

For these parents to successfully lead the way to a close and respect-ful family, they needed to break free of their bad habits. Patrick agreed to be more consistent in enforcing the family rules and more support-ive of Sherri, which she appreciated. In fact, I asked Patrick to become much more involved when Katie behaved disrespectfully, as this would take a lot of the discipline pressure off Sherri and help the two parents function more as a unit.

Sherri acknowledged that she needed to soften her style with Katie when making requests or redirecting her. Also their relationship needed some serious repair, so that weekend she took Katie out for a favorite mother-daughter activity they'd abandoned somewhere along the way: shopping and dinner. Katie was thrilled, and they both had a great time.

I taught Patrick and Sherri about the pour-it-on technique, and they started using it right away whenever they noticed Katie being respect-ful. (I wish I could have seen Katie's response the first time Sherri gave her a pour-it-on!) Sherri also found that when she suggested the right skill or used problem solving on the go rather than nagging or yelling, Katie responded much better.

Here's an example of the old demolition expert Sherri, as described by Katie:

Sherri:	(irritated) Katie, your room is still a mess. I thought I told you to clean it up yesterday.
Katie:	I will. Why don't you leave me alone!
Sherri:	Don't you dare talk to me like that, young lady. You

	march upstairs and get busy cleaning right now!
Katie:	All right already. Do you always have to shout?

And here's the new Sherri, putting her gardening skills to work:

Sherri:	Honey, I noticed your room still needs to be picked up.
Katie:	Oh yeah, I forgot.
Sherri:	I'd like you to get that done today sometime.
Katie:	I was going to see if Maggie could come over.
Sherri:	That sounds great. You can have Maggie come over after your room is clean. It shouldn't take you long at all.

Over several sessions with Katie, I taught her how to use fast listening, flexible thinking, and the STAR problem-solving steps. It turned out that Katie really did want to get along better with her parents, so she practiced these new skills and made a good effort at putting them to use. Patrick and Sherri saw that she really was trying, which gave them more pour-it-on opportunities. Katie quickly noticed that her dad had firmed up and her mom had softened up. Funny thing was, she liked it.

Sherri was no longer parenting like a demolition expert, and she and Patrick were now functioning as an effective unit. There were still rough moments, but Katie and her parents were able to talk them through in a much more respectful way. Patrick and Sherri were turning into gardeners, and their flower was starting to grow. Within about four months, they were well on their way to becoming a close and respectful family.

Watch Your Garden Grow

Like Katie and the other children whose stories I've shared in this book and like hundreds of other kids I've known, your child can learn that respectful behavior really does work out better than disrespectful behavior. He can experience the joy that naturally results from treating others the way God wants him to. Your entire family will benefit as well. As you train your child like a gardener, you'll find yourself once more truly enjoying him as you create happy memories together. You'll rejoice as you watch him develop respectful habits that will set him on the path toward becoming a respectful young adult.

God didn't give us children so we could tear them down; he entrusted them to us so we could nurture them like gardeners and bring out the best in them, helping them blossom into the people he created them to be. That's how we train our children to honor God in their daily relationships. That's how we teach them to treat others as they would like to be treated.

That's how we raise respectful kids.

- You can train your child like a demolition expert, or you can train your child like a gardener.

- If you train your child like a demolition expert, sooner or later you'll damage your relationship.

- A gardener plants the seed, waters it, and carefully pulls out the weeds without damaging the flower.

- When you train your child like a gardener, new respectful behaviors begin to take root and grow into habits that will shape her character and bless her future.

- God didn't give us children so we could tear them down; he entrusted them to us so we could nurture them and bring out the best in them.

1. Read Proverbs 16:32, 1 Corinthians 13:4-7, Galatians 5:22-23, and Colossians 3:12-14. What do these verses reveal about how God wants us to train our children?

2. How would you describe your parents' style of training?

3. Can you think of a time when you have responded to your child like a demolition expert? What impact did it have on your child's behavior? On your relationship? On how you felt about yourself?

4. Training your kids like a gardener involves three things:
   - Planting the seeds of respectful behavior
   - Watering those behaviors so they grow
   - Removing the weeds (disrespectful habits) that remain

   Which aspect of your role as gardener most needs improving?

5. Why is it so important to *carefully* remove the weeds, or disrespectful habits, from our children's lives?

6. As a leader and teacher that God has placed in your family, what one improvement do you plan to make to strengthen your family relationships and serve as a more effective model of respect?

7. How has this book influenced your overall parenting style?

8. Describe the most memorable concept you've learned from *Respectful Kids*.

Notes

1. Some children, for neurological or environmental reasons, exhibit negative behavior that is much more resistant to change than typical. These children will need help beyond the scope of this book, including individual and family therapy. Some may need to be treated with medication as well. If your child exhibits behavior that is extremely disruptive to your family, has threatened to destroy property, has made comments about hurting himself or others, or behaves in any way that causes significant problems at home, school, or with friends, please consult your family physician or a qualified mental health professional immediately.

2. *Merriam-Webster's Collegiate Dictionary*, 11th ed., s.v. "habit" (Springfield, MA: Merriam-Webster, 2003), 559.

3. *Brainy Quote*, http://www.brainyquote.com/quotes/quotes/a/aristotle145967.html.

4. The process of problem solving was originally developed by T. J. D'Zurilla and M. R. Goldfried in "Problem Solving and Behavior Modification," *Journal of Abnormal Psychology* 78 (1971): 107–126.

5. Despite my best efforts, I have not been able to identify who originally developed the STAR problem-solving acronym.

6. Dr. Ross W. Greene uses these same steps as one part of his approach for problem solving with explosive children in his helpful book *The Explosive Child: A New Approach for Understanding and Parenting Easily Frustrated, Chronically Inflexible Children* (New York: Quill, 2001).

7. John C. Maxwell, *Developing the Leaders Around You: How to Help Others Reach Their Full Potential* (Nashville: Nelson, 1995), 37.

8. Many thanks to Jeffrey Prater, PhD, my clinical child psychology professor at Fuller Theological Seminary, for his creative ideas on effectively using time-out, several of which are included in this chapter.

9. I first learned of the concept of positive practice as one component of a dry-bed training program developed by Azrin, N. H.; Sneed, T. J.; and Foxx, R. M. in "Dry-bed training: Rapid elimination of childhood enuresis," *Behaviour Research and Therapy*, 12, 147–156. My use of positive practice as a method of teaching and practicing respectful behavior is an adaptation of this concept.

About the Author

DR. TODD CARTMELL is a popular speaker and child psychologist who holds a doctorate in clinical psychology from Fuller Theological Seminary. He specializes in the treatment of a wide variety of childhood and adolescent disorders.

Thousands of parents have enjoyed Dr. Cartmell's humorous and action-packed parenting workshops at churches, parent groups, and conferences across the United States as well as internationally. Dr. Cartmell also has been a guest on numerous radio and television programs. His books include *The Parent Survival Guide* and *Keep the Siblings, Lose the Rivalry.*

Dr. Cartmell maintains a clinical practice in Wheaton, Illinois. He and his wife, Lora, live in Geneva, Illinois, with their two boys.

MORE PARENTING HELP FROM NAVPRESS.